Praise for *Why Johnny Can't Sell*

"Look in the mirror. You could be Johnny. Regardless of your age, or gender, you may have the wrong habits for sales success. This book contains the real-world sales success elements for every Tom, Dick, and Sally in sales. Buy it, and change "can't sell" to "sells like hell!""

Jeffrey Gitomer
Author, *The Little Red Book of Selling* and
The Little Red Book of Sales Answers

"If your reps are struggling to make the grade in today's highly competitive business environment, you'll discover why in this information-rich book. Plus, it's packed with powerful but uncommon selling strategies and tools to put Johnny back on the honor roll. I give it an A+."

Jill Konrath
Chief Sales Officer, SellingtoBigCompanies.com
Author, *Selling to Big Companies*

"*Why Johnny Can't Sell* will earn its place as an indispensable tool for sales reps, sales and marketing managers, and C-level execs who want to build a solid, productive selling process into their company cultures. Kantin and Nick are right on the mark with page after page of great insight, actionable advice, and a wealth of thought-provoking self-assessments that bring focus to the challenges faced by every salesperson. I especially appreciated the pragmatic treatment of sales tools and their role in a comprehensive and effective sales process. This is now required reading for our CRM sales staff and is a volume I will personally keep close at hand for ready reference."

Elvin J. Monteleone
Sr. VP & General Manager
Sage Software
CRM Solutions

"Nick and Kantin's work closes what was, until now, a glaring hole in how organizations tackle preparing a sales force for success. By putting *Why Johnny Can't Sell* and what it reveals to work, you will set your sales force up for success—don't miss this opportunity to get ahead of your competition."

Bill Byron Concevitch
Chief Learning Officer, Witness Systems
Author, *Counter-Intuitive Selling: Mastering the Art of the Unexpected*

"You must learn to sell if you want to survive—and more importantly, you must learn to sell *effectively* if you want to thrive. Find your competitive advantage in *Why Johnny Can't Sell*—this book will give the direction."

Howard Stevens
Chairman, HR Chally

"Any sales professional interested in adding value to their customers, their own company, and ultimately prospering from that activity, will learn much from this informative text. *Why Johnny Can't Sell* provides us with tools to assess our current state, relative to a competitive standard. *Why Johnny Can't Sell* will be required reading for our team."

Bob Knebel
Vice President, Sales, Bombardier Flexjet

Why Johnny Can't Sell

...and What to Do About It

MICHAEL NICK & ROBERT KANTIN

 **KAPLAN** PUBLISHING

President, Kaplan Publishing: Roy Lipner
Vice President and Publisher: Maureen McMahon
Acquisitions Editor: Karen Murphy
Development Editor: Trey Thoelcke
Production Editor: Caitlin Ostrow
Typesetter: Todd Bowman
Cover Designer: Jody Billert, Design Literate

Published by Kaplan Publishing,
a division of Kaplan, Inc.

Printed in the United States of America

06 07 08 10 9 8 7 6 5 4 3 2 1

Library of Congress Cataloging-in-Publication Data

Nick, Michael J.
    Why Johnny can't sell—and what to do about it / by Michael J. Nick and Robert F. Kantin.
        p. cm.
    Includes index.
    ISBN-13: 978-1-4195-3573-4
    ISBN-10: 1-4195-3573-0
    1. Selling. I. Kantin, Robert F. II. Title.
HF5438.25.N5264 2006
658.85—dc22

                                                          2006013035

Dedications

Michael J. Nick To the greatest loves of my life, Jonathan and Jessica, thank you once again for your maturity and patience during this process, I am so proud of you.

Robert F. Kantin To Marylee, my wife and fellow snow-skiing fanatic, for your unwavering love, encouragement, and support.

Contents

Foreword

On the Art and Science of Successful Selling

What if I asked, "What's your definition of selling?" What would you say? Would you say, "Oh, I know exactly what selling is all about"? If you are so sure, can you articulate some of the ideas that are floating through your mind at this instant? Can you frame a coherent sentence that begins with "Selling is . . ." What? Can you say it? Can you write it down?

If you happen to be someone who loves process, then your definition may begin with, "Selling is a process where buyer and seller agree on exchanging goods or services for money." Or, if you love helping people, you may define selling as Zig Ziglar does: "You can get in life anything you want, providing you help other people get what they want."

Take a moment today to ask everyone you meet in your sales organization, "What's your definition of selling?" Chances are that every single person will give you a different answer. The more people you ask, the more you learn about people's underlying motivations. Some people define selling as something that they do to people, instead of for people. Others define selling as a way to satisfy their relationship needs, their money needs, or their ego needs.

Well, here is the big idea. Your definition of selling is the DNA of your sales approach. Here is another big idea. If you have not consciously defined what selling is, chances are that you are equally unaware of your definition of success. Why? Like it or not, both definitions are intimately connected, like twins. Let me explain. I've asked hundreds of very successful salespeople how they define success. You can easily do the same, and I predict that you will find four distinct patterns. The first group of people defines success as having something, like a house in a prime location, a fancy car, a fast boat, or a second home. The second group defines success as experiencing a special feeling. This group says, "I am successful when I feel happy." The third group defines success as a process of setting and achieving their goals. Once they have reached a goal, they set bigger goals and work toward them. The fourth group defines success as finding their mission in life and fulfilling that mission.

Let's take Mary, a goal-oriented salesperson. Her definition of selling may be, "I define selling as helping people reach their goals." Bill may define success as moving up to a bigger house. He is likely to say, "I define selling as the ability to write my own paycheck." Bill's manager will probably say, "He's a good salesman, and he rides the company like a horse. He's a strong performer, but when the horse gets tired, he'll switch horses in a heartbeat."

Okay, so you think we've got this all figured out. Step one, define selling. Step two, define success. Step three, know your DNA, and this will help you become more successful. Wrong.

One insight isn't going to make you smarter or more successful. What will make you more successful is a lot more insight. *Why Johnny Can't Sell* is filled with insights, but it is not going to make you more successful unless you apply these insights. What stands in the way is the application of your own untrained imagination.

Take a deep breath right now and, as you inhale, think about these two words: "sales success." What comes to mind? Can you imagine yourself being a huge success in selling? Do you imagine yourself flying to an exotic destination, checking into a top resort hotel, walking into the ballroom in your best suit, hearing your name being announced by the CEO of your company, asking you to step on the podium to receive the Salesperson of the Year award, receiving a crystal trophy with your name engraved and the biggest check you've ever seen in your life?

Well, here is another clue to your destiny. Napoleon Hill once said, "What the mind can conceive and believe, it can achieve." The question is, why don't we invest more time conceiving a clear image of the kind of success we want for ourselves?

Dr. Michael Maccoby, the author of *The Productive Narcissist,* a book that describes the characteristics of visionary leadership, told me that we're all born with an instrument and that we need to find out what it is and learn how to play it.

If you find that you don't have any talent for selling, do yourself a favor and find another profession. If you are 100 percent sure that you have the talent for selling, then learn all you can to improve that talent to the highest level of perfection. Give it your 100 percent and visualize every day what sales success means to you.

Someone once said that selling is an art and a science. *Why Johnny Can't Sell* describes many scientifically proven steps that lead to success. Let me add a few thoughts about the art of selling. A great sales producer once told me, "Selling is like a performance. It's a work of art. And like any artist, I work very hard at making my art disappear." When I watched this salesman in action, I was impressed by his ability to suspend his natural drive to talk and present. He listened with extraordinary patience and displayed genuine curiosity in the customer's business issues. He did not advance any ideas or solutions until he was completely confident that he fully understood the customer's situation. He said afterward, "My first goal is to get my prospects to trust me so they can express themselves fully, freely, and frankly. I need to get them in a state of mind where they feel safe." When I asked why, he said, "Selling is all about change and people fear change. They fear the unknown. They worry about making the wrong decision.

They fear changing and failing. My role is to lead them safely, step-by-step, from where they are to where they want to be."

Another top sales performer once told me, "I compare the art of selling to jazz. I listen to a customer's riff and then I respond with a riff of my own." This salesperson explained that selling was a process of "cocreation." That definition works well with the one shared by Dr. Norman Vincent Peale, the author of *The Power of Positive Thinking.* He said, "Selling is a process where buyer and seller walk the road of agreement together."

The movie director Robert Altman once said that making a movie is like going to the beach and creating a sand castle. The waves ultimately wash away the castle, but the castle lives on in our memories. The same is true with salespeople who follow the process of cocreation. Their customers soon forget about the price of the product or service, but they do remember working with a great salesperson.

The hardest part of selling is not failure or rejection. The hardest part of selling is our inability to approach every sale as a blank canvas, without any emotional leaks that may spill over from a previous call. I once played golf with Gary Player, and after I hit a bad shot he said, "Don't worry about it, just focus on the next shot and treat it as a separate entity. Never allow the emotions from any shot spill over to the next one."

Let's go back to the world of art. The Italian painter and sculptor Alberto Giacometti once said, "What's essential is to work without any preconceptions whatever, without knowing in advance what the picture is going to look like. It is important to see only what exists." The reason many salespeople fail is simply because they don't uncover what exists. They either "read" something in the buyer's mind that was never there or they fail to hear what the buyer really said. A painter who steps into a landscape with the intent to paint a scene must first erase all other landscapes in his mind in order to see. Likewise, a good salesperson must approach each customer with a blank canvas.

The best advice I've ever received from anyone about success was from my aunt. She was a highly accomplished cook. She created award-winning pastry that was legendary in our family and our town. Every time she'd come to the dining room with one of her creations, she apologized, saying something like, "Oh, this chocolate cake didn't turn out so well, there was some problem with the filling, and the temperature of the oven wasn't just right." Of course, her cake was just perfect, like all the previous ones she served over many years. One day I asked her why she was always critical about her own work. She said, "We can't achieve perfection, therefore we have to be humble and always find ways to be creatively dissatisfied with our work so that we'll never run out of excuses for not improving."

Gerhard Gschwandtner
Founder and Publisher
Selling Power Magazine

Acknowledgments

Tom Hayes, thank you for your dedication and commitment to making this book great! It would have been difficult without you.

Bob Makowski, my friend whose life imitates art—with you around, I will never run out of material to write about. Thanks for everything.

Gerhard Gschwandtner, thank you for your support of sales as a profession and sales professionals throughout the world and, of course, for agreeing to write the foreword to *Why Johnny Can't Sell*. In addition, we would like to acknowledge Larissa Gschwandtner for working with us to get the cartoons into the book, compliments of and with permission from *Selling Power Magazine*.

Rob Schaefer, thanks for the ideas and input; Brian Sommer, for your incredible insights; Jim Kanir, for the sales process samples; Bill Byron Concevitch, Howard Stevens at HR Chally, Jane Richardson, Kendra Lee, Rob Schaefer, and Jill Konrath, for your thoughts, ideas, and input.

We also want to thank Jim Dickey for your research at CSO Insights; we appreciate your allowing us to use some of your data.

We would like to acknowledge the following customers, who helped us with our research: Gary Greenberger at Constructware; Gary Provo at eGistics; Bob Knebel at Bombardier Flexjet; Dave Hunkele at S1 Corporation; Linda Roach and Laurie Emerson at PlanView; Maya Natarajan and Gary Szukalski at Verity; and Dave Bracken at DMP; as well as VerticalNet Solutions, Pentawave, Penta Technologies, and Oracle.

Thank you to our agent John Willig at Literary Services, and Trey Thoelcke, our editor at Kaplan, and of course, Jessica Nick for taking my picture for the cover. Thanks to Nicki Fritz and Audrey Felske for your encouragement and support. Finally, thank you Marianne for allowing me to sit for hours and edit in your coffee shop.

Lastly, thanks to Michael Cunningham and Karen Murphy at Kaplan Publishing, for believing in this idea and helping us bring Johnny's story to life.

Introduction

We set out to write a book that could make all of us Johnnys better salespeople—and now you hold the results of that desire in your hands. Who should be reading it? Sales executives and managers who want to build a better team, CEOs who want to better understand why their Johnnies can't sell, salespeople who want to sell more and get (back) on top, and the maverick salesperson who simply needs more ideas on how to drive his or her sales manager crazy. We'll shortly come back to that in more detail.

Each chapter begins with Johnny's current challenge (we'll introduce Johnny in a moment) and goes on to discuss how you can overcome the challenge. A short summary recaps the ideas discussed.

This book begins with our observation that the bad habits we formed years ago continue to haunt us today. We point out how times have changed, and that what worked in the past just doesn't work now. There are many myths in selling. Johnny, like most sales professionals, tries to make himself believe many of the myths we discuss in Chapter 2.

These lies drive many of the excuses we hear each day in sales managers' offices.

Next we review the concept of consultative selling. There are literally hundreds of consultative selling approaches. Most of us know the major companies that provide consultative sales training: Solution Selling, SPIN, CustomerCentric Selling®, and Selling to VITO, to name a few. What most of us don't know is that there are hundreds of smaller boutique companies that provide the same type of training, but more customized to your issues, needs, and sales training goals—KLA Group, Selling to Big Companies, Pyramid Power Selling, and others. This is important for Johnny because he follows the methodology he learned from his previous employer. But his new employer follows a different one and follows it to a different degree than Johnny's old company. This could be a problem for all involved.

In the past, sales tools played a less major role in the sales process. Sales tools existed, but usually in silos or independently developed and used throughout the organization. ROI4Sales did a project in the late 1990s for Hewlett-Packard to build an ROI tool the sales force could use to differentiate itself from its closest competitor. The idea was good, but the execution stumbled because the ROI tool didn't integrate with any other sales tool HP used in its sales process. It viewed ROI as just one more event that sometimes took place as a prospect moved through the sales cycle. Throughout this book, we discuss the development, use, and misuse of sales tools. Just like HP, many organizations have these si-los of sales tools that their sales forces are developing, using, misusing, or not using at all. Johnny will need some help to tie it all together.

Johnny faces many challenges with prospecting, pipe-line management, and forecasting. He tries to deal with the irony that companies spend millions of dollars on technol-ogy each year to keep salespeople from selling to them—spam filters, voice mail, pop-up blockers, call screeners, and so on—yet we don't understand why our own sales force has difficulty contacting prospects. We have uncovered many techniques to help Johnny get through to the most difficult C-level executive. We tap the great minds in sales and mar-keting to help us break through these barriers.

In several chapters, we guide you through tying it all to-gether by helping you assess your existing sales tools and the gaps that may exist in your tool repertoire. We introduce a con-cept called *process connections information* (PCI) and the im-portance of using custom sales tools as sources and uses of this PCI. The book incorporates several exercises to help you iden-tify and map your unique PCI. Next, we show you how to use the road map to define gaps in your sales process or methodol-ogy and determine what has to be done to close them.

Finally, we provide a comprehensive resource guide to help you sell more. This guide will reveal companies, prod-ucts, and Web addresses of some of the best sales resources we could find in the marketplace today.

www.whyjohnnycantsell.com

Be sure to visit *www.whyjohnnycantsell.com* to order the *Why Johnny Can't Sell* Project Team Pack and other resources to help you assess, build, and deploy a set of sales tools that will help you close more deals.

How to Use This Book

There are many tables and figures to help you understand the concepts we discuss. In addition, there are helpful resources you can access on our Web site, *www.whyjohnnycantsell.com,* that tie in with these ideas. We encourage you to complete each of the tests, self-evaluations, and exercises. Don't make the mistake of just mentally doing the exercises. It will make a significant difference in your organization if you read the chapters in order and carefully fill in the tables and complete the exercises. By doing so, you'll experience a cumulative knowledge gain in two areas:

1. *Assessment:* Some exercises will help you understand your current situation. It's easy to talk about concepts, but it's more difficult to put things in writing. Therefore, various exercises will help you assess how closely you're following a consultative sales methodology and the effectiveness of the sales tools you're using (or not using).

2. *Application:* We designed other exercises to help you apply our concepts. Again, it's easy to read about concepts, but it's more difficult to decide how to apply them to your company and its products and services. You will find these exercises more challenging. We recommend that you don't skip any. Complete them all and in order. If possible, work with one or two people because we think most readers will benefit from a team approach.

Consider *Why Johnny Can't Sell . . . and What to Do About It* as your sales resource and reference guide as you develop your own customized sales tools and sales technique. And share this book with your corporate management team so they will understand why, without their commitment, Johnny can't sell . . . and what they can do about it!

Why Johnny Can't Sell from a Different Perspective

- *Sales Professionals.* We will provide you with several resources to make your job easier—books, services, and ideas on lead generation. Next, we'll help you understand how following a consultative sales process and using integrated sales tools can make a difference in your sales results. If you complete the exercises and fill in the tables, it will help you spot any gaps in your company's sales process. Many of these gaps you can fill. This book is not intended for you to start fixing major deficiencies in the organization because that's likely a significant undertaking, which requires management approval and support.

- *Sales Managers.* We will provide you with several resources to make your job easier—books, services, and ideas on training, managing, and coaching your sales team. We'll help you understand why your consultative sales strategy, processes, tools, and training must be completely customized and integrated. We'll help you identify the sources and uses of prospective customer information and the relationship of this information to sales tools. We'll give you insight for working with your sales professionals and reinforcing the need to follow your consultative sales methodology. Finally, we provide a road map to filling the gap between product training and sales training.

- *VPs of Sales.* We will provide you with several resources to make your job easier—books, services, and ideas on effectively managing and coaching a sales force. We will help you get an overall look at the effectiveness of your sales methodology, processes, tools, and training. By completing the exercises and filling in the tables with your sales managers, you will gain not only a gap analysis, but a road map to implementing many of the ideas presented, improving your sales revenue and reducing your cost of sales.

- *VPs of Marketing.* We will give you some insight into the complexity of your company's consultative sales methodology and all the things that must come together to sell your products and services. We describe many resources available to your organization that should help sales align with marketing in the development, customization, integration, deployment, and support of sales tools. We'll help you identify some opportunities where your expertise and that of your staff can help the organization, especially when sales professionals have to provide output to a prospective customer. Although it may be difficult for you to complete the exercises, we do feel you must participate in the process and strategy outlined throughout this book.

- *CEOs of Small Companies.* We will help you understand what's happening, or should be happening, in your sales department. We also will explain how and why your sales professionals should follow a consultative sales methodology. By completing the exercises, you can spearhead the effort to assess your current situation and help determine what is necessary to turn your sales force into a selling machine.

- *CEOs of Large Companies.* We will give you some ideas about how to evaluate the effectiveness of your

company's sales strategy, processes, tools, and training. We provide a road map for working with the VP
of sales to define a project and course of action for
correcting any deficiencies.

So have we accomplished what we set out to do? Only
time—and you—will tell. Feel free to contact us at
info@whyjohnnycantsell.com and share your experiences.

Meet Johnny

Johnny called us when he accepted a position as sales director for a new division of a 20-year-old company. His job
was to sell new products they were launching using their existing resources. Once the new division started selling and
showing results, he was told he could then hire a sales staff
and grow his division. His boss, Dave, used to be the VP of
sales but had recently been promoted to general manager.
Dave promised Johnny he would work with him to get the
new division launched, and Johnny would have support
from Sara, the VP of marketing, for lead generation and
marketing materials, and he would also be given use of the
corporate customer resource management (CRM) and sales
force automation (SFA) systems.

Johnny is an old friend of ours who has worked for several "hot" companies in the past. After a long and prosperous
sales career at IBM during the dot-com era, Johnny moved

to a venture capital–backed start-up as a regional VP of sales. He managed a small staff of salespeople who sold CRM systems. Johnny's team had fair success and went public just before the market crashed. Johnny cashed out and took a year off to get his head together. Upon his return to corporate America, Johnny took over as GM at a network services company and struggled with management over what he called "creative differences." Eventually, he was asked to move on. Finally, Johnny took over as VP of sales at a small software company and worked there for about a year before accepting this new position.

The compensation plan had the potential to double Johnny's income. And he felt he was a perfect fit for his new position. He had

- previous experience selling high-ticket hardware, software, and professional services at the C level;
- a proven track record meeting or exceeding sales quotas;
- consultative selling experience;
- good communications skills;
- a Rolodex of contacts from his previous employers; and
- experience building a high-quality consultative sales team.

1

Bad Habits
Are Hard to Break

"Your career seems to have plateaued."

Johnny had been very excited about his new company; however, when he called us, he was definitely feeling like the honeymoon was over. Johnny was continually disappointed with how the organization was preparing him to sell this new product line. Dave, Johnny's boss, claimed the corporation "follows one of the leading consultative sales methodologies" and insisted Johnny follow the tenants of the corresponding book to the letter.

After nearly a week in product training, Johnny learned a lot about the functions, features, and benefits of the company's products. But when Johnny asked, "Why would a person buy these products and services?" all he got was a technical discussion about features in the design. He didn't get anything about the issues, pains, or goals their prospects might be facing.

Johnny was working a few leads he managed to scrape together. He tried many of the prospecting techniques he used in the past like calling early or calling late. He even offered to take a couple of prospects to play golf or have lunch with no avail. Johnny quickly realized he needed to make some changes in the way he sells, as he was going nowhere. He decided to focus in on four primary sales functions: sales methodology, sales tools, integration, and developing a training program for the staff he was eventually going to hire.

In recent years, many organizations have found that their sales forces haven't delivered the results they expected. It seems that closing profitable sales has gotten more challenging, while the performance of top sales professionals has deteriorated. Certainly, the playing field has changed from the "irrational exuberance" of the mid-1990s to late 1990s. Selling seemed a lot easier before that bubble burst. Sales cycles were much shorter. Many companies purchased freely because they had extra cash from their recent IPOs or infusions of venture capital. Many of us saw or participated in the exuberance. Everyone was buying. Times were great—everyone was making quota and the "president's club" trips were fabulous!

Part of the reality back then was that some sales professionals simply took orders. We all remember the saying, "No one ever got fired for buying from IBM." It obviously wasn't that simple, but when the market was flush with IPO and VC money and the technology sector ruled, selling was definitely easier. It was what we like to call a "show up and throw up" environment. Some salespeople felt little need to understand a buyer's unique situation, critical business issues, or goals, much less the proposed solution's impact on the buyer's business. These salespeople didn't need to know exactly how their product or service was going to perform in the buyer's operation or affect their bottom line. Many of these past top performers were just very good at delivering presentations, demonstrations, and "feature dumps." We've probably all seen them in action.

Ironically, the "show up and throw up" approach worked for many sales professionals who were lucky enough to be selling the "hot" products or services. The economy was different (perhaps better) for buyers, and/or their buying habits were different. Whatever the reason, no one had to sell consultatively—salespeople were on cruise control and well compensated for it.

When "show up and throw up" works, some sales professionals might reason that buyers are evaluating all the top competing products or services. Therefore, they must be knowledgeable; they must know exactly what they need and why they need it. It really isn't necessary to get too involved. Just present the flash and sizzle and see if it sticks.

During the "irrational exuberance" era, many buyers had budgets and typically signed contracts if the products or services seemed to make sense for their organizations. After all, wasn't everyone buying? If they were not ready to buy, it was time to move on. There's another hot prospect around the corner, another presentation and demonstration to be done, and probably the next big order to write and commission to collect.

The reality is that those days are gone and probably will never return. Many bad sales habits were born, and three key factors contributed to today's sales reality:

1. Past economies and changed buying processes
2. Fallout from the 1990s—where only the rational survived the "irrational exuberance" era

3. Inadequate consultative sales training, process, skills, and lack of integrated sales tools

Past Economies and Changed Buying Processes

In the mid-1990s to late 1990s, when the economy was really growing, companies had less stringent budget and purchasing policies. Many managers could buy whatever they wanted as long as they had the dollars in their budgets. You might say that anyone could have been a sales professional back then. And this economic ripple effect touched us all. Of course, this "irrational exuberance" came tumbling down when the dot-coms started disappearing like mocha lattes at Starbucks.

Even though the economy has rebounded somewhat, buying processes have changed. Many veteran sales professionals, at least the ones who are still around, often can't make quota as easily as they did in the past. Instead, their bad habits and lack of skills or sales training led to these familiar excuses across sales managers' offices:

- "We need to cut price; we're too expensive."
- "It takes forever to get a decision."
- "They need more time to evaluate the impact of our product (or project) on their operations."
- "They won't return my calls or e-mails."

- "They don't seem to understand what they need, or they simply don't understand how our product (or service) will make a big impact on their business—even after my demos!"

The reality is that in today's economy, even though it is better, selling is more difficult. It's more competitive, more complex, and sales cycles are more protracted. Some companies simply refuse to spend the budgets they have or can't buy because it's not in this year's plan. But the companies with budgets who are able and willing to buy aren't readily buying because a lot of vendors and their salespeople aren't prepared to sell.

Fallout from the 1990s—Only the Rational Survived

After the 1990s, the surviving companies started (or continued) to spend budgeted funds only after completing in-depth analyses of the proposed products or services—probably because these companies have always been more rational and less exuberant. These companies have always needed to understand exactly how a proposed solution would work in their unique environments. They closely scrutinize a seller's value proposition and benefit statements. More important, these buyers expect sales professionals to do much more than deliver a presentation or

"I see you made this month's issue"

demonstration. They expect that any sales professional who wants their business must first

- understand their uniqueness—which can mean current operations' critical business issues, key pains, and their implications, as well as improvement opportunities, needs, and objectives;
- define the exact application of the proposed product or service to their situation;
- identify the available financial and nonfinancial benefits they will receive if they buy—the required value proposition; and

- explain exactly how the selling organization will install or implement the proposed product or service.

The reality is that many companies don't prepare their salespeople to operate in this more demanding, buyer-focused sales environment. They may provide product or service training, but that often doesn't translate into meaningful quantitative business benefits for their buyers. Other companies don't follow a customized, repeatable consultative selling methodology, and as a result, their sales professionals don't have the skills needed to analyze a buyer's business environment and make value-based recommendations.

The bottom line is today's buyers expect sales professionals to be more like business consultants, trusted advisors, or partners, and less like vendors. Buyers have the expectation of a long-term relationship with the selling firm. Those sales professionals who haven't or can't make that transition are off to new opportunities, or soon will be. Selling organizations that have yet to identify the need to make a change may still think selling is a numbers game; 100 leads translates to 10 qualified prospects which results in 3 closed sales—the idea of "just get more leads and work harder and anyone can make quota" is not a reality any longer. Companies with this attitude simply aren't preparing and equipping their sales professionals to win.

Inadequate Consultative Sales Processes, Skills, and Tools

Many companies have bought consultative sales methodology books and seminars, the books and speakers who offer big ideas on how to connect with a prospect, but the companies fail to follow through with putting the theories into practice. As a result, their salespeople don't have a clear road map to success. What typically occurs is that, after attempting to make the generic methodology and sales tools work for them, salespeople return to a "what worked in the past" approach, and ultimately fail. The "build it and they will come" mentality is one of the past. According to "Sales Effectiveness Insights 2005—State of the Marketplace Review" by CSO Insights, about 60 percent of a sales force achieves quota. *An organization's lack of commitment, direction, and focus on the sales process, method, and tools is a primary factor in the failure of its sales force to achieve its goals.*

Selling organizations inadvertently contribute to this by providing what they think are high-quality training courses. What they end up with is superficial consultative sales training. For example, companies will send their new salespeople to a four- or five-day public sales training seminar and expect that, upon their return, they will magically become consultative sales professionals. While these public seminars provide excellent consultative sales basics, they are unable to impart the skills needed to use the techniques to sell their company's products or services. Public seminars have to be generic to work for the broad spectrum of attendees and the industries that they represent. The majority of these public seminar organizations offer customized courses tailored for companies.

Most sales professionals leave these public seminars feeling good about their newfound knowledge and are eager to use it on the job. Nevertheless, they find it difficult to apply this new knowledge to selling their specific products or services to a real buyer. After a month, they will have forgotten 80 percent of what was covered in the seminar. Perhaps the VP of sales should send all new sales professionals to Las Vegas—they would probably remember more about the experience, and their morale certainly would be higher. With a 20 percent retention rate after the first month, the seminar, like Las Vegas, ends up being little more than high-priced entertainment.

A good friend recently returned from a four-day Solution Selling™ course. When asked what he thought of the course, he said, "I enjoyed the course. However, it is only good if management buys into it and continually reinforces the message. They need to manage to the concepts and methodologies we were taught. Also, I believe we need to supplement and integrate the training with sales tools we discussed during the week. The course spent little time, if any, on things like selling value or customizing the sales tools we use throughout our sales process." The reality is, his organization will not customize the material and will not build sales tools to supplement the training course. Research indicates that tools such as letter templates, value estimation systems, sales proposal models, and prospect intelligence systems are not developed in concurrence with sales process training courses.

Stuff You Need to Remember

The 1990s were no doubt a time of "irrational exuberance," which we may never see again in our lifetime. However, the lessons we learned from this euphoric buying period should be carried on from generation to generation. The profession of sales has changed. Clinging to bad selling habits or a reliance on what worked in the past will likewise ensure you a profession change. But if you embrace the change and learn from the past, you will be well prepared to succeed.

✓ The days of "show up and throw up" are over, and consultative selling is necessary for complex sales situations.

✓ Organizations have found that their sales forces haven't delivered the results they've expected. Closing profitable sales has gotten more challenging, while the performance of top sales professionals has deteriorated. The playing field has changed, and sales cycles are much longer. Several factors account for this phenomenon: changes in buying habits;

fallout from the 1990s; and inadequate consultative sales process and skills, combined with a significant lack of integrated sales tools.

✓ Companies now buy only after completing in-depth analyses of the proposed solution. They need to understand exactly how the solution will work in their unique environments.

✓ Selling organizations need to customize their sales methodologies and continually reinforce a consultative sales approach; they need to develop custom sales tools, systems, and processes that help to reinforce their methodology.

2

Stop Lying to Yourself: Myths and Realities

"Son, take it from someone who's been selling for thirty years. The best way to win over new clients is to buy them a meal."

Dave gave Johnny a copy of the consultative selling book the corporation used and followed. A classic best seller, the book had been around for more than a decade, and though Johnny had heard of it and its premise, he had never actually read it. Having been formerly trained in a different sales methodology, Johnny didn't think it would be a big deal to learn another. At his last job, they used an outside consultant to customize their sales methodology and integrate it into their sales process, as well as link it to several sales tools. Johnny thought he could do this on his own.

Johnny took the book home and quickly finished it over the weekend. Although the jargon was different in the new book, it looked similar to what he had learned in past sales training courses. The book began with how to identify the buyer's "pain" and quickly moved to using his product's features and benefits to resolve that pain. The book discussed how to match up the buyer's and seller's needs and how to deal with objections. The templates in the back of the book provided a basis for gathering generic customer data that could be used with other sales tools yet to be developed by Johnny. The following Monday, Johnny and Dave sat down to figure out how they were going to use the book within their complex consultative sales environment.

We believe it is important to have a basic understanding of what your company is selling. Is it a commodity or a complex product or service? Is price and availability the most important factor to your prospects? Or are they more interested in solving their business problems, satisfying their needs and objectives, and defining the value proposition provided by your product or service? When selling complex products and services, sales professionals must have different skill sets and tools than those used by someone selling commodities.

For a better understanding of the nature of your company's products and services, see the exercise in Figure 2.1. Enter Commodity or Complex depending on which sales process characteristics most closely reflects your company's product (or services) and sales process.

If, after completing the exercise, you have written more in the Complex column, then reading this book and completing its exercises can help you better understand why you or your sales team are part of the 40 percent not achieving quota. In addition, you'll be better prepared to identify gaps you may have in your company's consultative sales methodology and to design and develop consultative sales processes, skills, and tools that can result in dramatic sales improvements.

If you have more in the Commodity column, then this book can help you be more competitive utilizing tools typically used in a complex sale. The sales tools and analysis described throughout this book will enable you to present your products, services, and value in a manner rarely used in a commodity sale. This differentiator will help ensure you achieve your quota when your competitors are still struggling.

FIGURE 2.1 Commodity or Complex?

COMMODITY-TRANSACTION SALE	COMPLEX SALE	COMMODITY OR COMPLEX?
Simple product or service—perceived as a commodity by the buyer	Complicated product or service	_____
One- or two-call close—perhaps telesales	Multiple consultative calls, demonstrations, and presentations—perhaps technical sales support required	_____
Fewer than two decision makers	Multiple decision makers—executive committee or board-level decision	_____
Low-risk decision for the buyer—a wrong decision will have minimal impact on the business	High-risk decision for the buyer—a wrong decision could adversely affect the business	_____
Relationships less important—buyer views the sales professional as a vendor	Relationships very important—buyer may view the sales professional as a business consultant or partner	_____
Product or service quality viewed as similar for all suppliers	Product or service quality closely linked to characteristics, reputation, and attributes of the selling organization	_____

FIGURE 2.1 Commodity or Complex? *(Continued)*

COMMODITY-TRANSACTION SALE	COMPLEX SALE	COMMODITY OR COMPLEX?
Implementation or installation not critical or irrelevant	Implementation or installation a key concern	_____
Technique selling	Value-based selling	_____
Price quote	Proactive sales proposal or response to a Request for Proposal (RFP)	_____
Price and availability more important	Return on investment (ROI) very important or required	_____

Myth: We Don't Need No Stinking Consultative Sales Methodology

There are many top-notch consultative sales methodologies available from which to choose. Each methodology has an approach that may appeal more to one company and its sales force than another. Though all of these methodologies are unique, they do have some core process similarities:

- A sales professional needs to gain an in-depth understanding of the prospective buyer's unique situation and environment as it relates to the product or service being sold.

- By selling consultatively, the sales professional needs to develop skills that demonstrate business acumen, and as a result the prospect may view him or her more as a business consultant, trusted advisor, or partner and less as a vendor.
- The sales professional must demonstrate how the proposed solution will meet or exceed the buyer's needs, objectives, and goals.
- Selling consultatively builds a long-term, higher-margin, and mutually beneficial partnership between the buyer and seller.

Consultative selling is more demanding in that it requires the seller to understand the buyer's business issues, pains, and goals. The seller expects the buyer to evaluate the proposed and available options on the basis of value and return. This give-and-take negotiation is the reality of selling consultatively.

Myth: Emotional Connections Are for Sissies

Most buying decisions are based on emotion. We typically buy on emotion and attempt to justify our decision with logic. If you ignore this emotional connection between buyer and seller, and buyer and product, even this book won't help you. If the buyer simply doesn't like you or your products, this or any book won't help. If, however, you have established a relationship as a knowledgeable consultant or trusted advisor, read on; this book will help you develop the necessary processes, tools, skills, and metrics to make you a successful consultative sales professional.

Myth: I Can BS My Way through Any Sales Call

If your sales professionals cannot tell you how they utilize the corporate consultative sales methodology, then the idea of your company having a consultative sales methodology is a myth. For example, a friend of ours started a new job, was sent to a generic public five-day customer-centric sales course, and was expected to make the leap from selling the fictitious widgets in class to selling complex IT solutions to Fortune 100 companies back in the real world. If sales professionals can't tell you how to use their methodology's guidelines, processes, and tools to sell the company's products or services, then are they selling consultatively? If our friend spends five days in a seminar yet doesn't have one custom sales tool that supports the consultative sales process when he gets home, how can he sell consultatively? How can he begin to implement the methodology if his management doesn't reinforce it? Sales professionals aren't selling consultatively if they're just talking as if they are. They're just *talking the talk* not *walking the walk*.

The 2005 CSO Insights: "Measuring Effectiveness" report (*www.csoinsights.com*) reveals that only 12.6 percent of sales professionals surveyed closely follow a formal sales methodology. Of these 12.6 percent, 68 percent achieved their quota (significantly higher than average). This doesn't seem like rocket science to us. Companies that follow a consultative sales methodology and hold their sales force accountable for the results will close more business. We wonder why more companies don't get on the bandwagon—it just makes sense. Maybe they need some rocket scientists on the sales force.

Reality: Questions Are Critical to a Consultative Sale (aka Two Ears and One Mouth, Use Them in This Proportion!)

By following a consultative selling methodology, sales professionals know the right questions to ask and when. In the book *Conversations on Customer Service and Sales,* Brian Tracy points out, "The customers only enter the sale when they realize that they have a need, and up until the time that *you ask them the right questions* and uncover the problems, and suggest perhaps that they could be better off in a cost-effective way, customers are usually not interested." A consultative selling methodology will ensure you are not wasting an executive's time gathering useless information. When our friend returned from the customer-centric sales course, he had an assignment to complete several solution development prompter templates

(SDPs). Developed by CustomerCentric Selling®, an SDP is a template that collects information to formulate diagnostic questions as they relate to an event, player, and action. With SDPs, our friend can now customize his selling approach upon his return to work.

If your salespeople don't know whom to question, what to ask, or how to word the questions to sell your products or services, they're not selling consultatively. Asking generic questions doesn't count and doesn't work. Sales professionals need to ask questions that elicit the right information about the prospect's current situation and the potential application of the proposed product or service in the prospect's unique business environment.

The custom application of the consultative sales methodology may be more important for a company and its sales force than which methodology it selects. This may sound like heresy, but the point is a company must ensure that its salespeople adhere to a customized consultative sales methodology. The methodology must fit what they sell and how they do business—custom, not generic, is the key point. Some companies combine pieces from several methodologies to create one that works specifically for the way they do business—that's okay as long as they document the methodology and develop the custom sales tools needed to support it.

Does your company provide its sales professionals with custom sales tools that reinforce your custom sales

FIGURE 2.2 Consultative Selling Competency

Does your company provide its sales professionals with:

	YES	NO
Customized value estimation tools for each of your products or services?	—	—
Custom sales proposal models for each of its products or services?	—	—
Consultative sales training based on your company products or services using its custom sales tools with company-specific case studies, simulations, and exercises?	—	—
Custom CRM/SFA tools designed to be integrated with both your sales process and sales tools?	—	—
A sales intelligence system for your team to search for help on sales activities?	—	—

methodology? Complete the survey in Figure 2.2 to assess your level of consultative selling competency.

If you answered "No" to all or most of the questions in the survey, and you still think your sales professionals are selling consultatively, they're not even close. They're probably not even "talking the talk." As a result, your company may be missing opportunities or losing deals because it hasn't prepared or equipped your sales professionals to be more engaged and consultative with their prospective buyers.

If you answered "No" to more than two of these questions, you are working against the investment you made in your sales methodology. It's very simple—like a puzzle needs all the pieces to complete a picture, you need all the pieces to complete the sale. For example, a prospect might request vendors to provide a value-estimation breakdown complete with total cost of ownership (TCO) and return on net assets (RONA). If Vendor A provides a credible and objective ROI model, including TCO and RONA, and Vendor B provides a mocked-up spreadsheet touting ROI calculations, whom do you think will win the business?

Reality: Connecting the Dots Is Critical

Sales is the untamed frontier of the business world: unpredictable, passionate, theatrical, full of eccentric characters, and dangerous to the newcomer. Like the frontier, the destiny of sales is to be explored, settled, and tamed by people using the right tools and technology. But many also will perish on this frontier, because they are unprepared, unnecessarily exposed to the elements, and annihilated by quick-footed and aggressive foes. The real question is: how many bones will lie bleaching in the desert or buried on Boot Hill before the new era finally arrives? And will you be one of those victims?

Tom Siebel, *Virtual Selling*

Siebel's quotation (and his book) remains one of our favorites to this day—it cuts to the heart of why sales professionals will always fail without the right tools and technology. Organizations spend millions automating, training, and throwing money at sales programs. We have yet to see a consistent, repeatable approach to integrating process and automation into a single system. Where are the "best practices" for sales process? Many have tried, like Siebel Systems, Oracle, and SAP, but no one has put it all together. If you look at accounting systems, for example, AR, AP, GL, and payroll all work together to create the financial reports, best practices, and general accounting principles (GAP). There is no such integration when it comes to sales tools. Organizations should carefully select, customize, and integrate their sales methodology, sales processes, and sales tools so their sales professionals are totally prepared to compete.

Myth: We Lose Because We Aren't the Cheapest

If you truly believe that the cheapest sells the most, we have a lot of work to do. In a complex sale, the future of selling requires believing value will ultimately prevail in a competitive situation rather than relying on the traditional practice of price slashing. Most agree no matter what price you sell your product or service for, someone will always sell it for less. It is the value that you add that will determine whether a customer succeeds or fails in

"I remember now—you were the company that always had the lowest price."

their implementation. Johnny will never be successful selling purely on price alone.

Reality: Decision Makers Hide Behind Technology

It's ironic how we spend millions of dollars isolating our executives from salespeople using technology, yet they complain when their own sales force can't get through to other executives. In Chapter 4, we discuss how to use technology to beat the technologies that are keeping us from selling.

Reality: Information Is Power

When an organization integrates its consultative sales process with other supporting processes, it is forced to develop custom sales tools to support its sales activities—for example, a prospect questionnaire, confirmation letters, value estimation tools, and proposals. These sales tools incorporate prospect information that links the analyzing, presenting, and proposing processes to each other. We call these prospect information links process connections (discussed in depth in Chapter 5). Process connections are important because without them, you cannot integrate your consultative sales methodology's processes to your custom sales tools.

Process connections information represents the most important prospect information a sales professional can gather to sell a product or service. If you are selling complex goods and services, you will ask questions throughout the sales process that identify

- decision makers,
- stakeholders,
- issues, pains, and goals,
- chain of pain (or the ripple effect of an issue on your colleagues),
- current cost of the situation, and
- potential solutions.

Each piece of information that you gather you will use repeatedly in sales tools such as your sales intelligence system, SFA system, ROI or value estimation analysis, system configuration, and, of course, your proposal. You do not have to reinvent the wheel each time you use a sales tool in the sales process.

Myth: Once a Sales Superstar, Always a Sales Superstar

In the book *Conversations on Customer Service and Sales,* Ken Edmundson tells us, "Mathematically we have a 52 percent chance of hiring the right person if we just flip a coin, and studies reveal that we only increase that a whopping 8 percent by using our wonderful interviewing skills." So what does this tell us? Why don't we just hire anyone off the street? What Ken goes on to say is there are certain traits great salespeople possess. They include:

- Passion
- Determination
- Self-discipline
- Attitude
- High self-esteem
- Belief system
- Communication skills

Note that history of success is nowhere on this list. Johnny's success in the past doesn't really matter going forward. There are many tools in the marketplace to evaluate sales talent. We suggest you employ one or more sales-force evaluation or sales-candidate screening companies, such as HR Chally Group (*www.chally.com*), to increase your odds of hiring the right person for the job. Howard Stevens, CEO of HR Chally, told us in a recent interview, "There are three things you need to do with great salespeople: first get out of their way; second, get distractions out of their way (reports, internal issues, etc.); and third, keep them in sales." Moving them into management is a big mistake many organizations make.

Stuff You Need to Remember

In this chapter we laid the foundation for many of the reasons why Johnny can't sell. Johnny has lied to himself about his ability to prospect, qualify, and close. This new organization had Johnny take a personality test, and the results were more accurate than Johnny wanted to believe. He felt he used consultative selling to capture the critical information needed to manage a sale. Johnny believed he could leverage corporate to access decision makers, and besides, Johnny was a superstar before, of course he'll be a superstar here too.

Johnny is not entirely in control of his fate. Corporations that provide sales training and product training rarely provide the link between what you sell and how to sell it. Specifically, why do people buy these products or services? What is the value you deliver? Who is your "perfect" prospect or target? The lack of a custom link will result in a gap that forces sales professionals to fall back on techniques they used in their past. That link needs to include sales tools that integrate and connect with the process and sales methodology. For example, we strongly suggest you embrace a sales methodology, customize it to your environment, integrate it with your sales process, and develop custom sales tools to support it. If organizations provide their sales force with the tools, processes, and methodologies, it still doesn't ensure success. Corporations still need to hire the right people with passion, discipline, self-esteem, attitude, good communication skills, and a belief system, and train them . . . a lot!

It is imperative to stop lying to yourself. The economy has changed; the way people buy has changed; and the profession of sales must change with it. Ask yourself:

- ✓ Do I sell a commodity or a complex product or service?
- ✓ Am I (or my sales force) selling consultatively or just "talking the talk"?
- ✓ Do I (or my sales force) have these seven traits?
  - – Passion
  - – Determination
  - – Self-discipline
  - – Attitude

- – High self-esteem
- – Belief system
- – Communication skills

✓ Do I believe people only buy the cheapest?

✓ Do I respect a person's time when I am able to ask him or her questions?

✓ Do I understand the need to connect processes (sales process, proposal process, presentation process, etc.)?

✓ Are our sales processes all integrated with our sales tools?

3

Morphing Into a Business Consultant

*"Marsha, why did we ever tell our
sales manager we were quick learners?"*

After several months with his new company, Johnny was sent to a five-day consultative selling course (based on the book Dave gave him) with other new salespeople from corporate. Remember, corporate sells a different product. Johnny was looking forward to this course, so that he could learn how to use the book's techniques, which included advice on creating new opportunities, qualifying prospects, and managing the sales process. Johnny also had questions for the instructor on value estimation, sales intelligence, and (his personal struggle) getting people to call you back. Johnny also wanted help with forecasting. From his previous experience in other jobs, Johnny knew they were rarely accurate. The book discussed the idea of "controlling" the sale, which sounded intriguing, if vague.

Consultative selling has been around for decades. It's not a new concept, and it comes in many styles and colors. Most sales professionals could easily list some of the prominent consultative selling methodologies. For the sake of this book, we will define consultative selling in three distinct, yet integrated, parts. Consultative selling means a sales professional

1. analyzes, understands, and confirms a buyer's unique business environment and operations, including issues, pains, goals, and the cost of status quo;

2. prescribes ways to improve the buyer's business by reducing costs, avoiding costs, and/or increasing revenue; and

3. assists the buyer to make an informed decision about purchasing the seller's goods or services.

Part 1: Analyzing the Buyer

Analyzing the buyer is often the most difficult and challenging part of a consultative sales process because it requires effective interviewing techniques, communications skills, product knowledge, and business acumen. A consultative sales professional, at a minimum, must

- begin the bonding experience—establish an emotional connection;
- establish credibility;
- identify the buyer's business issues, pains, and goals;
- determine the current cost of status quo; and
- define and understand the buyer's specific tactical needs and strategic objectives.

We recommend the following sales tools for analyzing the buyer's current situation. This isn't a complete list, but it is a good start for assessing what you may have, want, or have access to and do not necessarily use (a more complete list is available in the Resources section):

- **Custom sales analysis worksheet,** designed to gather current situation information

Great Plains (now Microsoft CRM group) hired us to develop a customer questionnaire for its distributors to use throughout the sales process. With more than 2,000 distributors at the time, the requests for Great Plains resources were exhausting. Known for its superior support, Great Plains needed to standardize the information flow from the distributors to the support staff providing assistance. We established its objectives and began an extensive interview process of the staff, distributors, and development personnel. During our discovery, we quickly realized that developing a set of questions to ask throughout the sales process would not turn these distributors into subject matter experts. The questions alone would not drive credibility into the sales process unless they had meaning and purpose. If you ask a question for the sake of asking a question, you show disrespect for a prospect's time, and waste your time, as well.

We took a different approach to its request. We gathered the reasons people buy CRM systems and identified the associated issues, pains, and goals. We documented all of this information in a matrix. This matrix served as a foundation for the issues the industry faced, not necessarily the issues Great Plains

(Continued)

resolved. Next we reviewed each issue with the Great Plains marketing team and determined what features resolved the issue, pain, or goal. This information was documented in the same matrix. We analyzed this data looking for the quantitative value Great Plains could deliver. Questions were then developed to capture data as it related to the issues that we knew Great Plains could resolve. Each question had a purpose to capture a current situation or the cost of status quo.

- **Custom ROI valuation tools,** used to collect current information and apply estimated value of potential solutions
- **Sales intelligence systems** to research and store buyer trends and strategy, industry information, and competitive analysis
- **Financial reports** on a prospect's Web site, 10K, annual report, and so on
- **Subscriptions to business contact databases** (e.g., Jigsaw.com, Harris Infosource) to collect information on your prospect
- **Confirmation letters** to confirm the data gathered and establish credibility by proving you understand your prospect's issues, pains, and goals

Integrating sales tools into your sales process is a primary key to success in developing a solid foundation for selling consultatively. Why Johnny can't sell is due in part to his lack of consultative sales training and skill, yet his lack of integrated sales tools is fueling his frustration and potential demise.

Part 2: Prescribing a Solution

After identifying the prospect's critical business issues, analyzing its current situation and receiving confirmation from the prospect's team, a consultative sales professional will prescribe or formulate a recommendation for resolving the identified issues. The sales professional must

- determine, with the buyer's participation, how the proposed products or services can deliver value in the organization's unique business situation;
- Calculate with the buyer its value proposition, including an analysis of how your proposed product or service will reduce costs, avoid costs, or increase revenue; and
- describe and demonstrate how the proposed product or service would best be implemented for the buyer.

Depending on the complexity of the product or service you are selling, you would likely have had to demonstrate or prove your product's or service's ability to resolve the buyer's critical business issues. Here are a few sales tools you may find useful when working through this phase (see the Resources section for additional information):

- **Sales intelligence systems** to perform research on resolution strategy, configurations, pricing methodologies, and industry trends. This tool can be used and updated by any personnel throughout your organization.

- An **ROI valuation tool** customized to the specific product or service being sold to calculate the current cost of the status quo and estimate the financial benefits the buyer will realize.

- A **feature-benefit conversion** customized for each product or service that helps to define the nonfinancial benefits a buyer might realize. These intangibles should not be used in your financial analysis tool set but reserved for the proposal. To create such a document, we suggest a customer survey. No one knows better than your customer base the perceived value they have received.

- **System and price configurators** to determine and confirm correct product configuration.

- **CRM systems** to store information captured and ensure product availability and price.

- **Confirmation letters** to confirm financial and nonfinancial benefits the buyer should realize.

- A **planning questionnaire** to define resource requirements for the implementation or installation. Gather your implementation and support teams together and develop a list of questions needed for a smooth transition from sales to training and postsales support.

Take another look at this list. How many of these sales tools will you have to create and/or customize for your sales force? You're right. All of these sales tools have to be custom.

Part 3: Assisting the Buyer to Make the Decision

With the consultative sales approach, you are able to produce a paradigm shift in the relationship between buyer and seller. The seller becomes more of a trusted advisor or consultant, not just a salesperson. This transformation does not occur magically. The set of skills the seller must take on to be credible includes: product knowledge, the ability to apply the product knowledge to the buyer's current situation, customer insight, experience, patience, and good communication skills.

A consultative sales professional must be able to articulate a proposed solution. Paint a picture the buyers can relate to; they need to project themselves into the picture you are painting. Buyers need to "feel" the presentation. When discussing their issues, pains, and goals, make the hair on the backs of their necks stand up!

To assist the buyer in making an informed decision, you must provide several deliverables created throughout the sales process. The sales tools we discussed in "Part 2: Prescribing a Solution" represent information sources for producing documents used by the buyer to make an informed decision. This part of consultative selling is where the rubber meets the road. The difference between winning and losing is often determined by the quality of these deliverables. How many of these sales tools does your organization provide its sales force?

- Up-to-date and accurate customer case studies
- Customer reference lists (available to call or visit)
- Confirmation letter templates
- Current situation report, including cost of status quo
- Custom ROI or value estimation tool
- Custom sales proposal models
- Custom Microsoft® PowerPoint® presentations
- Financial summary and dashboard of proposed solutions
- Value review document, used to measure value delivered postsale

Again, all of these sales tools have to be customized for your company and its products and services. You will struggle selling anything using generic sales tools.

Misconceptions about Consultative Selling

There are several misconceptions about consultative selling:

1. Salespeople are born with consultative selling skills.
2. Consultative selling takes the relationship out of the sale.
3. Consultative selling originates with product development people.
4. Consultative selling must reside only in the sales department.

Natural-born Salesperson: Yeah, Right

The first misconception, that salespeople are born with consultative selling skills, is total rubbish. In the previous chapter we discussed the seven primary traits a sales professional needs to succeed. They included passion, self-discipline, determination, attitude, self-esteem, a belief system, and communication skills. If you find a person with these traits and no sales experience, hire him or her! Training and custom sales tools obviously play a major role in the success of a consultative salesperson. However, if a candidate has these personality traits and sales tools, and the company provides a quality, integrated training program, he or she will succeed. Sales professionals are just like athletes: a very few have natural talent (Michael Jordan, Pelé, Wayne Gretsky); the rest have to study, train, and work hard to be the best.

To reach a level of success selling, like a professional athlete, you must sacrifice a portion of your life to your craft. The most successful sales professionals typically read more sales books, attend sales workshops, receive newsletters, and try new techniques. They don't believe sales is a numbers game, they believe sales is about helping people with their problems. There are many studies that prove sales is not a natural-born talent, but an acquired skill.

Time to Kiss and Make Up

Another misconception we often hear is that consultative selling takes the relationship out of the sale. The reason this is brought up is because consultative sales typically includes a team sales approach and a standard set of questions. This is construed as less "relationship" selling and more detail gathering. Actually, it's quite the opposite. Selling consultatively means sales professionals have to put significant effort into understanding their buyer's needs. This means they must spend time with the buyer asking questions and learning about the business. Remember the paradigm shift that is taking place? By selling consultatively, buyer relationships become long term.

There are tools and techniques to assist you in continuing your relationship with buyers, even after the sale. Many of these tools you can develop on your own. For others, you may want to enlist the help of a professional organization. We recommend a 360-degree sales approach. This means, once you have sold your product or service, return a year later and measure the success your customer has experienced. This is a more detailed use of the quantitative questions you asked during the sales process. Compare your original success criteria (quantitative questions and goals established to define success) to their current situation. In the book *ROI Selling* (Kaplan Publishing) I discuss the 360-degree ROI. This concept enables you to use ROI and value estimation during the sales process up to the close, and then return at a predetermined time after the sale and measure the success of your implementation. Not only will this 360-degree concept ensure a better long-term relationship with your customer, it will differentiate you from your competition. Our research indicates that less than 5 percent of sales professionals return to a customer and measure success. This is not good for long-term relationship building.

If you are following a consultative selling approach and maintaining your customer relationships based on the information you gathered during the sale, you should experience longer customer relationships and lower customer attrition rates.

Look Inside the Fortune Cookie

A third misconception about consultative selling originates with product development people who often say, "The sales team doesn't understand our products well enough to sell consultatively." The fact is some salespeople don't have in-depth knowledge of their products because it requires specialized technical skills. Therefore, consultative selling often must embrace a team-sell approach. Organizations such as Oracle, SAP, IBM, and HP have developed sales departments that include sales professionals, presales, and product or feature specialist positions. While the primary function of the presales personnel is to specialize on a product suite, their knowledge must go beyond product information. They need practical (business) experience applying the product to the buyer's issues, pains, and goals.

This is where we see a problem with some corporate training programs. These training programs focus their efforts on helping the individual with one-on-one selling skills. There is a lack of flexibility in the training programs to teach a team sales approach. Keep in mind, there is a difference between training a team and team training. Training a team properly should include the relationship-building aspect of consultative selling.

Stand in the Cold in Your Underwear

A final misconception is that consultative selling resides just in the sales department. Developing a successful sales strategy for your company requires input and participation from every part of the organization—marketing, development, human resources, customer service, product fulfillment. Sales professionals should know that they can't market, sell, collect, deliver, and support customers by themselves. In other words, if your company sells consultatively, then other departments should get involved in the process. For example, professional services might need to be involved in establishing implementation time frames; or you might ask marketing to help design a branded binder and divider tabs for your proposals.

To be a successful consultative selling organization, you need to drive consistency in the customer relationship. Customer attrition is very costly to an organization. It means losing ongoing revenue (maintenance, training, etc.) and upselling opportunities. It also means acquisition costs to replace a lost customer.

Are You Morphed Yet?

Take the following short test to evaluate how effectively your company has implemented a consultative selling methodology. No one is looking at your score, so be honest when you answer these questions.

1. Which consultative sales methodology has your company implemented?

2. When was it implemented?

3. Did every department send representatives to the training?

4. Does your entire organization promote and follow the consultative selling approach?

5. How did your company implement the methodology? Engage the consultative sales process vendor, an outside consultant, or use internal resources?

6. On a scale of 1–10, 10 being very effective, how effective do you feel your consultative selling implementation is going?

7. What was done to customize the methodology for your company?

8. List the major activities, deliverables, and sales tools that were customized to match your company and its products or services.

9. Briefly describe the initial rollout and training program for your company's sales force. Identify duration of program, exercises, materials, etc.

10. How does sales management evaluate the ongoing use and effectiveness of the consultative sales process by the sales force?

11. What percentage of your sales professionals don't follow the methodology? What are the major reasons for not following it?
12. Do you think your company reinforces its consultative selling methodology?
    - If yes, how does it reinforce its use?
    - If no, what needs to be done?

This self-test is designed to make you think about your commitment to developing and deploying a custom consultative selling approach. It should help guide you through some of the areas of improvement on which you may need to focus. Once you complete the test, ask yourself, "Do the answers show me a road map for success?" Do you have complete company commitment to develop the strategy, process, methodology, and sales tools required to succeed selling consultatively? Are you building or establishing best practices?

Here Is Why You Fail

If your company follows a consultative selling methodology, you know it takes discipline, practice, and hard work. You also know that implementing and then sustaining a consultative sales methodology may not always succeed. Here are some reasons companies have failed to implement and/or sustain the implementation of a consultative selling methodology:

1. *Lack of senior or sales management support.* Management did not attend the initial training classes or participate in the development strategy. They may only fund minimal training and probably haven't developed custom sales tools or engaged vendors or consultants to help with the implementation. There are no provisions for managing the process or for follow-up and further training. This reflects "show up and throw up" management.

2. *No customization of sales tools.* A company implements a consultative sales methodology without developing custom sales tools needed to link its sales process to its products and services. As a result, sales professionals try to use generic tools or are forced to develop their own. This is like buying a sports car without the tires—it might look good and be a nice place to sit, but you're not going anywhere.

3. *Failure to reinforce the methodology.* This reflects management's failure to instill discipline within the sales force. Management may only focus on results while ignoring the methodology and the means and sales tools needed to get the results. When management doesn't consistently reinforce the methodology, sales professionals can and will skip or poorly execute defined sales activities or skip the use of sales tools.

4. *Inadequate new sales professional training.* Product and sales training is critical to sustaining a consultative sales

methodology within the organization. Sending Johnny to a public sales training seminar after spending a week in product training is a prescription for disappointment and, likely, disaster. Rather, all new sales professionals should receive custom sales training as it relates to the products and services they will be selling, including the use of all the company's custom sales tools. This typically requires a custom internal training program. Alternatively, the company can use outside resources who are certified in the organization's custom training program. When this is done effectively, a company can integrate sales and product/service training into a single program where sales, support, training, development, and management participate in the process. Consultative sales training must include the commitment of your entire organization.

If implementing a consultative selling methodology in your company has failed, make a list of the reasons and evaluate why. Or if you think the implementation of the current consultative process may fail within your company, try to identify what your company can do to avoid the failure or minimize the risk.

Figure 3.1 is an example of a chart that each of your sales professionals and managers can complete. Collect them and compare the results to each other, paying particular attention to duplicates. If you receive several of the same reasons

FIGURE 3.1 Reasons and Risks for Failure

REASON FAILED OR RISK FOR FAILURE	HOW TO AVOID OR MINIMIZE
Example: VP of sales who was instrumental in implementing the process resigned. New VP of Sales thinks relationship selling is more important—doesn't like all the work.	*Example:* If the company's management wants to continue its consultative selling methodology, then the VP of sales job description and qualifications should clearly define it as a requirement. Also, management should investigate the candidates' experience and commitment in this area during the interview process.

for failure or risk of failure, obviously you will need to address the concern.

Self-Assessment

Take a moment and assess your current situation as it pertains to your consultative sales methodology (see Figure 3.2). We use this information in later chapters. The horizontal axis indicates your level of customization for your current sales tools. Rate your company on a scale of 1–4. Did you hire a consultant to customize the training? Did you simply attend a public seminar? Do you have an ongoing custom program for training? The vertical axis indicates the commitment of your management team to the use and promotion of a custom sales methodology. Commitment includes

FIGURE 3.2 Methodology Assessment Chart

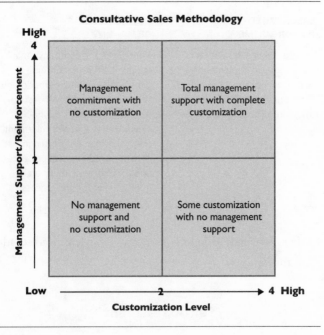

financing, attending training, incorporating the vernacular into reports. For example, if you currently use a hybrid of methodologies, and have no custom training and no commitment from executive management, then you would likely fall into the bottom left quadrant. Please take a moment and rate your company on a scale of 1–4 in terms of management's commitment. Add these two ratings together. The higher your organization rates on the scale, the better your opportunity for success in sales.

Score Analysis

- **0:** Your organization lacks adequate sales methodology customization and management commitment to really be a successful consultative selling candidate.
- **1–2:** Although you are making strides in either commitment or customization, there is still a major lack of both to make much of an impact on the sales process.
- **3–4:** You have gained momentum and have an opportunity to succeed. Pull it all together and identify what you need to create a complete customized program or additional management support and commitment.
- **5–6:** You are on your way to a very successful career. You still have a lot of customization to do to be successful. Be aware of silo projects (projects performed without management knowledge or support, or integrated with other sales tools and projects) when this occurs.
- **7–8:** Excellent job! You are on your way to a very successful sales career. Remember though this is only one component to sales success.

Stuff You Need to Remember

Consultative selling means analyzing, prescribing, and assisting the buyer to make an informed decision. There are many tools available to help the seller perform these activities. Each sales tool gathers information that is potentially used by other sales tools to produce the documents that keep the buyer and seller on the same page and the sale moving forward. Each document plays an important role in the consultative sales approach.

- ✓ There are many misconceptions about consultative selling; however, to successfully implement and sustain customer relationships a company must realize consultative selling does not reside only in the sales department.
- ✓ Consultative selling enriches the customer experience; it does not take the relationship out of selling.
- ✓ The implementation of consultative sales methodologies fails in companies for several reasons, including
  - lack of management support,
  - no customization of sales process components,
  - failure to constantly reinforce the methodology, and
  - inadequate new sales professional training.
- ✓ To effectively use consultative selling in your organization, you must subscribe to a methodology, customize the training and sales tools, integrate the process, and command management support.

4

Beat Technology Before It Kicks Your Butt!

"I'm working on a hot lead. He said he definitely was 'kinda–sorta' interested."

Having to start a division from the ground up, Johnny fo-cuses primarily on building a pipeline of potential customers. He spends his day following up on company-generated leads, which isn't much, just a handful that come into corporate through its Web site, direct-mail responses, and advertising programs. Johnny looks for some "low-hanging fruit" by contacting existing corpo-rate customers for the company's main products, but the limited access to decision makers is frustrating. Johnny begins each day with a call list of potential prospects. Although cold-calling is not his forte, he feels he has to get some activity going. His old boss al-ways said, "Busy gets busy"—which basically means that if you are busy doing something to generate business, other business will find you. In the past, Johnny had a knack for getting to executives. He would build a relationship with an administrative assistant, call early, call late, or even over the lunch hour. With all the tech-nologies getting in the way, these techniques rarely if ever work. He is finding fewer people actually answer a telephone these days, as he bounces from voice mail to voice mail. As for e-mail, Johnny has found that many high-level executives have multiple e-mail accounts or don't check their own. Assistants or spam filters often thwart his e-mails. Johnny needs help generating leads and break-ing down the barriers keeping him from getting to decision mak-ers. Johnny's days are filled with frustration.

Voice mail, spam filters, and number blockers are all technologies designed to stop salespeople from selling, and yet they make us personally more efficient. Many technologies drive a more efficient office and at the same time, make it more difficult for a salesperson to be effective. Your organization has probably designed and deployed a wall around your decision makers to keep them focused on the task at hand. It is ironic how we isolate ourselves from salespeople and yet complain when we can't get hold of someone we want to sell to.

Aside from the technologies used to prevent unwanted solicitations, there are many other challenges that Johnny faces: call screeners, rising travel costs, flight delays and cancellations, and of course his need to understand his own customer base. In today's selling environment, it is necessary to use innovative techniques and technology to beat the technology that's keeping you from selling.

A VP of marketing for a major pharmaceutical company told us that in any given week he gets "roughly 150 to 200 unsolicited calls" for appointments. That is about 10,000 calls a year. He had no choice but to use technology to keep salespeople away from him. He employed call screeners, e-mail filters, and voice mail to fend off the unsolicited contacts. He then related this story to us about his own sales force. "We have doctors in some cities charging our drug reps a fee of up to $175 for a 15-minute sales call. This doesn't stop the onslaught of sales calls doctors get every day. There are doctors who come in on their day off and meet with drug reps one after another. They are just lined up outside his office ready to pay their money for a 15-minute, face-to-face visit." But at least his salespeople get face-to-face meetings with the doctors. Many of us never get in the door or past security to talk to a decision maker.

Bring the Mountain to Muhammad

There is a saying: if you can't get Muhammad to the mountain, bring the mountain to Muhammad. We have never heard a salesperson say, "Everyone calls me back . . . I never have trouble getting hold of a decision maker." We have all experienced the frustration of being unable to talk to prospects. They don't take our call, return our call, or respond to e-mail. With all of the technology out there limiting our access to decision makers, we are forced to get creative. If you can't get to them, make it easy for them to get to you. Here are some commonsense ideas to generate leads for your sales force.

Web Seminars (Webinars)

The past few years have seen a rise in the number of online Web seminars. Tim Sullivan, from Sales Performance International (Solution Selling), tells us, "The best return on our marketing dollar for lead generation is the online seminars. We are running them twice monthly on various topics." Web seminars are a cost-effective way to generate leads, educate the market, and create demand for your products and services. Marketing for an online seminar is typically handled through "opt-in" e-mail campaigns (undoubtedly a low-cost way of getting your message out). The expense for the technology to conduct a Web seminar is reasonable; however, we encourage you to shop around. We have had good experiences with Go-to-meeting and Microsoft's Live Meeting. Another option we have used on a much smaller scale is Glance Networks (*www.glance.net*). There are also many free conference-call sites if audio is all you need. Our favorite is *www.freeconference.com.*

Blogs

One of the fastest-growing sales tools on the market is the blog. A blog is a *Web log,* a kind of diary that you (the blogger) allow others to read and comment on. Many corporations use blogs for employees and customers to learn more about their products, uses, successes, and, of course, failures. According to the article "Blogs Can Boost Sales" in the September 2005 issue of *CRM Magazine,* "The most common usage is self-promotion, an external blog where company insiders talk about products and events in a humanized voice." The article further explains, "Developer journals with fresh and frequent updates give the participants a stronger air of integrity and credibility." As a salesperson, you may think blogging is impossible; however, it is a very low-cost way of presenting and expressing your thoughts and ideas as they relate to your products and services.

Online Newsletters

Attracting prospects is much harder than it used to be. They are overwhelmed with e-mails, pop-up ads, junk mail, and cold calls. Jill Konrath, author of *Selling to Big Companies* and an expert on getting past the kinds of barriers thwarting Johnny, told us her company gets the majority of their leads from their own online newsletter. This is an incredibly effective tool, as your outreach is enormous, your content should be polished, and it can be relatively inexpensive to create and maintain. We personally subscribe to more than 30 weekly online newsletters. Some of the more popular ones we recommend are *Selling to Big Companies (www.sellingtobigcompanies.com), Bitpipe (www.bitpipe.com), Selling Power (www.sellingpower.com),* and *SalesAdvantage (www.salesadvantage.com).* Anyone can create an online newsletter. Microsoft Business Solutions has several reasonably priced services to create and manage online newsletters.

A hidden opportunity within your own grasp is your customer base. You have a gold mine of opportunity right under your nose and often don't realize it. Developing a tool to return to your existing customers and measure the value delivered, or simply survey their current situation is a nonintrusive way of upselling and cross-selling goods and services. Many organizations attach a goal or budget to achieving a percentage of their total revenue from their customer base.

Online newsletters, blogs, and 360-degree selling (see Chapter 3) approaches to your customers will ensure you receive your share of revenue from your existing customers. Siebel Systems to this day surveys its customer base annually and ties a percentage of every employee's bonus to the outcome.

Targeted Fax Campaign

A method for conducting surveys that can also be effective in generating interest is a fax campaign. Offer a white paper or research results if the person contacts you. Fax numbers are very easy to get. You can simply look on a prospect's Web site or call the front desk and ask for the fax number. Unlike an e-mail that can easily get deleted, a fax is typically placed in the recipient's in-box. There are many online fax companies you can use right from your computer. Here are two:

1. eFax—*www.efax.com*
2. Send2Fax—*www.send2fax.com*

Persistence Pays Off

If you have difficulty getting your customers and prospects to call you back or return an e-mail, try some of these tips to bring them to you. Each suggestion is a cost-effective technique to generate interest in your products or services:

- Conduct a Web seminar
- Build a blog
- Create an online newsletter for prospects and customers
- Develop a targeted fax campaign
- Create a customer survey or use a 360-degree selling approach

Get Muhammad to Come to the Mountain

Begin your prospecting approach with your own Web site. Your Web site must include information on the value you deliver. We recommend offering downloads that will draw prospects to your site. These downloads may include case studies, video clips, brochures, sample products, templates, or even games.

Instant Messaging

The use of instant messaging (IM), or chat technology, has expanded into a wonderful customer support and inquiry tool on Web sites. We visit many Web sites while performing research. Sometimes we can't find what we're looking for. We recently visited *www.oncontact.com,* a sales force automation tool company. While browsing the site, a chat window popped up and asked, "May I help you?" At first we thought it was a pop-up ad. Then we realized a person was at the other end, there to help with our questions.

Many organizations are using this technique for support. On Contact has brilliantly extended it to sales.

Search Engines

The Internet is the number one tool in the world for research. Search engines make it easy to find almost anything on any topic you can imagine. These powerful tools can also help you find leads. Use a search engine to research potential prospects. Enter keywords into the search engine and review the results as potential leads. Our favorite search engine is Dogpile (*www.dogpile.com*). Dogpile compiles results from Google, Yahoo, and MSN.

The "Rude" Letter

Multiple phone calls, e-mails, and faxes are proving to be unsuccessful for Johnny. However, one prospect looked pretty good. Johnny spent several hours on the phone discussing the prospect's issues, pains, and goals, followed up with a demonstration, and finally offered a proposal. But then Johnny couldn't contact the prospect again. It was as though his prospect fell off the face of the earth. Johnny tried to contact this prospect more than 30 times in 90 days. He could not get the prospect to respond to e-mails, voice mail, or even an overnight package. Finally, out of frustration, Johnny discussed this next move with his GM. They decided to create the following e-mail and send it to the prospect:

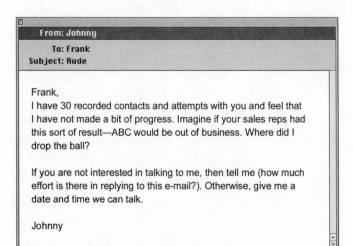

Johnny's e-mail got Frank's attention! Frank sent back the following message:

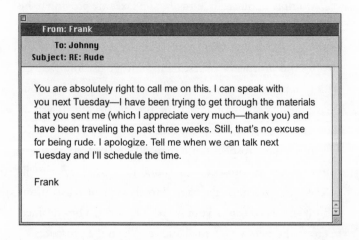

This story is absolutely true. (We changed the names, but not the text.) It is generally in our nature as human beings to not treat people rudely. Arrogance aside, rude is simply rude, and you have every right to call a person on it. Johnny did the right thing, and so did Frank. We do, however, strongly suggest you use this technique sparingly. It can backfire too.

Michael's Dad Says "Shock 'Em"

Michael's father (the salesman) once schooled him on how to effectively use a form of shock in the sales process. He said, "If the deal is stalled and the prospect is not responding, you have to do something (good or bad) to get his attention (shock him) and move him off the dime." In the above example, Johnny's e-mail is a shock technique. Over the years, we have heard of all sorts of crazy things. One company sent out a cereal box overnight with all of its literature glued to the back. The message on the package read, "Tomorrow morning at breakfast while you are eating this yummy cereal, please check out the back of the box." It worked, and the salesman got a call back. As salespeople, it is the unknown that drives us crazy. You must keep deals moving forward through your pipeline or you will never be able to close business or predict revenue. Michael's dad also said, "The one thing that will affect your stock price and job security is the inability to predict revenue." He has proven to be right on all counts.

The Book Review

An interesting technique we have stumbled upon is the book review. Yes, as odd as it seems, there are people out there advertising their companies through book reviews. Here is how it works. Sign up at one (or more) of the online book retailers. Be sure to include your real name, title, and, of course, your company name. Then, as you read books on sales, write a review. Others who have similar interests will see your review and perhaps visit your Web site to better understand what you do. Be sure to include in your review a hint of why and how the book affected you and your sales efforts. Amazon, for example, polls the reader on whether the review was helpful or not and publishes the results.

Book reviews are also a great source of leads. Go to one of the online book retailers and look up books about your product or service. Read the reviews and pay particular attention to people writing the reviews. Yes, the reviews contain prospects for you and your products. They list the contact name, title, and company. Obviously, these people are trying to make themselves better at their craft by reading the book they're reviewing. If you have a product or service that's appropriate for one or more of the reviewers, look up their contact information on their Web site and place a call to them, reminding them about the review they had written and what it is that you can do for them.

Aside from Amazon, our favorite online book retailers include *www.barnesandnoble.com, www.800ceoread.com,* and *www.booksamillion.com.*

The Secret to a Successful Sales Career Is Knowing Something No One Else Knows

One of the most valuable assets you can have is industry data. Gartner, PricewaterhouseCoopers, Aberdeen, and the like have made millions of dollars on their research. Readers like you have paid millions of dollars for the data they have collected. You also have a customer base and hopefully a database of prospects. You have the ability to conduct research and offer it to your prospects for participation. Many organizations have developed surveys to generate leads for their sales force. A simple e-mail campaign or Web site can be created to create a series of questions that can help both you and your prospects better understand the current state of affairs in your industry. We have interviewed companies that keep a database of all the data sales professionals collect during the presales questioning process. The data is then used in their presentations, ROI models, and proposals to show current industry trends and project future action. As part of the consultative sales approach, knowing the data will make you a more valuable asset to the prospect, as well as drive credibility.

Research Papers

Along with research, we highly recommend the use of white papers. If you are capable of writing a paper that can create awareness or help people assess their current situation, then you have a document that can be used to generate leads. In some cases, you may want to use other people's research papers. For example, our original paper, "Why Johnny Can't Sell" (available at *www.roi4sales.com/downloads.php*), is distributed by Microsoft to generate leads for its CRM products and services. If it is something people want, build it or borrow it, and they will come. We offer a variety of papers and assessment tools that draw hundreds of leads regularly. We offer them for download in e-mail campaigns, outbound calling blitzes, and during Web and in-person seminars. Most of our public appearances include some offer for research or a paper to drive awareness and demand for our products and services.

Be Accessible

When you leave the office, forward your phone calls to your cell phone, your e-mail to your Blackberry, or both to some other device. Nextel (Sprint) offers a cell phone with walkie-talkie capabilities. One of our clients in Chicago uses this technology to stay in constant touch with developers, managers, and contractors working off-site. We worked on a project for this company last year, and they supplied us with one of these phones so we could bypass voice mail and e-mail. Most of our work was performed over 90 miles away in Milwaukee, Wisconsin, but when we had questions, help was just a press of the button away. With all of the technology offerings to make you more accessible, there is simply no reason to miss a phone call or e-mail.

Remember, if you are having difficulty getting people to call you back, first make sure you are accessible. Second, try and contact people in good faith. If you must leave a message, be sure it is tactful, succinct, and to the point. Here are a few other books that may help with breaking through the spam-filter, e-mail, and voice-mail quagmire:

- *Cyber Rules* by Thomas Siebel
- *The Sales Bible* by Jeffrey H. Gitomer
- *Success Secrets of the Online Marketing Superstars* by Mitch Meyerson
- *Phone Power* by George R. Walter

Getting to the "Right" Contact

Today's selling organizations reside in every corner of the earth. Many markets are just beginning to boom. China, for example, is on the rise. We expect another technology boom as companies throughout the world rush to sell into the Chinese market. Establishing operations in China will be cost-prohibitive for most organizations. Therefore, the organizations unable to expand into this new market will be forced to use technology to carry their message forward. Technology exists today to transfer calls anywhere in the world, to transfer e-mail to personal devices, uplink video via satellite, and enable video conferencing; and with the up-and-coming Voice-over-Internet Protocol (VoIP) technology, as well as Video-over-Internet Protocol, the global communications options are limitless and dropping in price almost weekly. Johnny doesn't even need to leave his house to do a presentation for someone in, say, Enid, Oklahoma, or Beijing, China.

Corporations spend millions of dollars annually purchasing lists for sales and marketing campaigns. Our research indicates the best of these lists are approximately 60 percent to 70 percent accurate, and most do not provide e-mail addresses. Johnny's attempt to contact decision makers from a list that is incomplete and inaccurate is a waste of time and energy. Jigsaw Data Corporation (*www.jigsaw.com*) is a company that offers a business contact marketplace.

Through its Web site, you can buy, sell, and trade business contacts with other sales professionals. What sets it apart is the accuracy of its data, guaranteed fresh (within 30 days). The company currently has over 3 million contacts and are growing at 11,000 new contacts per day. While you still have to deal with call screeners, voice mail, and spam filters, services like Jigsaw still save enormous amounts of time by identifying who is the best contact and providing the correct contact information from the beginning. Another interesting company we came across in our research is Executive Link, which researches executive-position issues, pains, and goals in more than 40 vertical markets. A salesperson will now have insight into the top challenges, primary responsibilities, leading trends, and hot topics most on the mind of an executive or decision maker.

Sales Intelligence, There Is No Substitute

Johnny, like many new employees, has many questions about his new organization but doesn't really know where to go to get them answered. He asks his colleagues and sales administrator, but finds their direction leads to dead ends within the company. He is once again frustrated by the lack of sales intelligence within the organization. We recently spoke with Lisa Cramer, president and COO of Involve Technologies. Lisa tells us, "There is so much data stored in people's heads, and really no way of transferring this

knowledge cost-effectively and efficiently throughout the
organization. When you are a subject matter expert within
your organization, there is a good chance a high percentage
of your time is taken up by answering questions from others." Lisa points out corporations need to give their sales
force "easy" access to the following information:

- Competitive data and analysis
- Customer success stories
- Contract terms and conditions
- Training gaps and how to fill them
- New product introductions
- Key pains for companies in similar industries

Street Smarts™ (*www.involvetechnology.com*) is an innovative tool that enables sales personnel to "capture shares of
knowledge and disseminate know-how." Simply put, sales
intelligence systems give a person access to all the best practices, subject matter experts, and sales intelligence data
through a sophisticated search engine that is easy to use. It
launches right from your e-mail or SFA system.

There are many tools available to help you determine
who should be contacted within a corporation. We are not
big advocates of cold calling, yet research indicates over
70 percent of companies still perform cold calling. We are,
however, strong supporters of developing a precall strategy.
Tools like Jigsaw, Executive Link, and Street Smarts will
help develop good prospecting habits and a blueprint to a

successful sales process. Remember, even when you do get to the decision maker, you must employ solid consultative selling techniques.

Adapting to Change

There are many emerging technologies designed to stop us all from selling. This is not unlike the game of golf. As golf skills and equipment improve with every decade, golf course owners are forced to make their courses more challenging to keep them competitive. To offset advances in equipment (the new breed of golfers and their new Big Bertha™ driver), golf course owners add trees, make the greens faster, and put in fairway bunkers and sand traps. In the game of sales, the buyers have similarly changed the rules of the game, and the sellers must use their skills and technology to adapt.

Beginning in the next chapter, we start to analyze your current situation. We begin with introducing the term *process connections*. Process connections is the information that represents prospect data gathered and used throughout the sales process. This is critical to understand so you can identify gaps in your sales tools, sales process, and, perhaps, sales methodology.

Stuff You Need to Remember

There will always be challenges in selling. We are simply programmed to avoid a "salesman." Every time we enter a Best Buy store and get approached, we hold up our hands and say, "Just looking." Then, five minutes later, we turn around and look for someone to help us. We love to buy, but really hate being sold to. What we learn is, we all want to buy on our own terms, and timing is everything. With that said, how do we make it easier for Johnny?

✓ Use technology to beat technology.
✓ Focus on your message, using tools to draw your prospect to you.
✓ Stay engaged with your customer, using techniques like a 360-degree selling approach, customer surveys, and referral programs.

Techniques and technologies are much like bell or S-curves; they have a life cycle in which they will be copied, overused, and abused over time. This chapter discusses what is hot in 2005 and 2006. You will need to look at technology as it advances and stay ahead of the curve to get and keep a competitive edge.

5

PCIs: The Stuff You Need to Know and Use

"What you'll need for me is an honest face when talking about the products and a straight face when talking about our prices."

On completion of the five-day consultative selling course, Johnny was determined to customize the sales process to align with the new organization's sales goals. He quickly realized how many sales tools he needed but didn't have. Johnny started by developing a precall planning worksheet to be used prior to the first call. He referred to the sales training course materials and the templates in the back of the consultative selling book to help him with the design. He downloaded his prospect's 10K and annual report, and looked up the data stored in Dun & Bradstreet to determine what he could learn prior to the first call. In addition, Johnny tried to develop a series of qualifying questions that would help weed out unqualified prospects faster. Finally, he thought about competition. Johnny's previous employer had a marketing person who researched competition and provided up-to-date sales info. Johnny needed some background on the competition to help him develop a strategy and a stronger sales approach. These new sales tools served as the basis for building other sales tools Johnny would need later in the sales process.

Consultative Sales Process

Obviously, the most popular consultative selling methodologies have more than these three steps. Typically, they have multiple phases with a clearly defined sequence of activities, sales tools, and deliverables for each. As a starting point, we'll introduce our own generic process to show how and when different categories of prospect information are gathered. Our generic sales process has eight phases, some of which may have familiar-sounding names:

1. *Target*—Identify prospects that meet target market criteria.

2. *Qualify*—Hold an initial prospect meeting to determine if the prospect meets the minimum marketing criteria—e.g., enough revenue, enough employees. In other words, are they qualified to buy from us?

3. *Meet/Greet*—Conduct further meeting(s) to identify critical business issues—key pains, impacts, needs, and goals—and establish the cost of doing nothing.

4. *Presentation*—Present solutions that resolve the prospect's critical business issues. Then mutually determine the estimated value you can deliver.

5. *Proposal*—Formally propose and present the solution to the prospect, presenting ROI, total cost of ownership (TCO), and potential nonfinancial benefits.

6. *Due Diligence*—Customer evaluates proposal and validates proof points to make an informed buying decision. Check references, case studies, and legal review.

7. *Close*—Negotiations and contract signing.

8. *Postsales*—Conduct a sales process debriefing (win-loss analysis) and postsales value measurement.

Figure 5.1 shows how a prospect's interest in the seller's product increases and decreases as it and the sales professional move through the eight phases of the consultative process. The horizontal axis is time (our enemy in sales), and the vertical axis is interest. Notice how interest begins to decline as you move further into the sales process. Once your prospect has all questions answered, has reviewed the suggested solution, and has the investment information, the prospect will either close, buy from someone else, or, likely, do nothing.

Losers Never Learn

Each phase requires the salesperson to gather, process, and/or use different categories of prospect information. Obviously, a salesperson's knowledge about the prospect is cumulative. For example, to understand how the proposed product will work for the buyer, something that happens in the presentation phase often is dependent on information gathered in the preceding phases.

A salesperson can't skip over the information requirements of one phase as he or she moves through the sales cycle without creating information gaps—missing prospect information needed in a subsequent phase or phases. Neither can a sales professional skip phases to accelerate the process. For example, a salesperson can't begin the process by delivering a proposal because it would have little or no prospect information, no defined issues, pains, or goals, and no value estimation information in it.

FIGURE 5.1 Consultative Sales Process

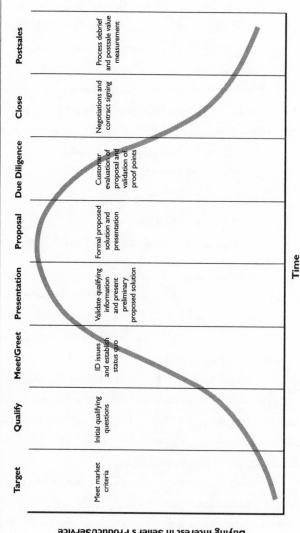

We've seen companies with sales processes that include the delivery of a sales proposal on the first sales call. We classify these as "boilerplate" proposals—the proposals are the same except for the name and perhaps the price. If your company follows this type of sales process, you might consider firing the entire sales force and implementing an online ordering system—otherwise, you need to realize that you have a very expensive proposal distribution system that's simply delivering price quotes.

Competitive Power— Prospect Information Links

The more time a sales professional spends with a prospective buyer, and the more questions asked and answered, the more knowledge he or she gains—unless the sales professional's not asking the right questions or capturing the right information. Sometimes certain categories of prospect information are needed to initiate the next sales phase. For instance, a sales professional can't complete the presentation phase or perform an ROI without identifying, capturing, and confirming the prospect's key issues, pains, and goals. Obviously, this is not rocket science.

Common prospective customer information often links sales phases and sales tools. We call this common customer information *process connections information (PCI)*. There are several reasons it is important to understand PCI and its linkages:

- The PCI linkages between sales phases enables and ensures a logical progression of prospect information-gathering throughout the sales process.
- Defining the PCI linkages between sales processes and sales tools assures the required information is gathered at the appropriate times and available for use when needed, either by another sales tool or in subsequent sales process phases.
- When identifying gaps in a custom sales tool kit, one needs to understand the PCI that links individual sales tools to each other and the availability requirements of specific PCI throughout the entire sales process.

Customer relationship management (CRM) and sales force automation (SFA) systems should contain some of the process connections information gathered and used during the sales process. In Tom Siebel's book *Virtual Selling,* he states, "In the future, the value of a corporation will be best measured by its knowledge of its customers, its knowledge of markets, and its knowledge of its own products. Therein will lay the company's competitive power." By including process connections information in your CRM or SFA system, you can

- facilitate or reinforce the consultative sales process,
- provide a prospect information database for the entire organization to access,
- develop high-quality best practices for customer correspondence and other sales process documents,

FIGURE 5.2 Integrated Process

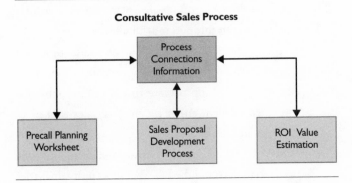

- compliment your market analysis and provide detailed feedback to marketing,
- capture market information used to assess sales strategy and goals, and
- complete a more accurate sales forecast.

Tying It All Together

In Figure 5.2 we see PCI integrated with the consultative sales process, an ROI valuation, and the proposal development process. While you could depict the PCI in a separate database within the consultative sales process, in reality, it's usually contained in various documents and systems, or in the minds of others throughout the organization, including the salespeople.

Note that each of the sales tools in this diagram (precall planning worksheet, sales proposal, and ROI value estimation) are typically used in different phases of the sales process. A precall worksheet is used early in the process, in the target or qualifying stage. The ROI valuation is used from the qualify stage through the close, and the proposal is used primarily in the proposal stage. So it's important to keep track of when process connections information is gathered and used—another reason to follow a consultative sales process.

We reviewed a product called Street Smarts from Involve Technologies. This sales intelligence system allows users to query information from sources within and outside their network, from department desktop computers to the Internet, for example. Such information can include pricing, competition, processes, procedures, employee information, or whatever your data administrator wants to make available to the sales force. We see this as an evolving technology that can potentially revolutionize and broaden a sales force's information pool. See Figure 5.3 for how the process connections information gathers the information from multiple sources and overlaps with the CRM, SFA, and sales intelligence repositories.

FIGURE 5.3 Stored Information

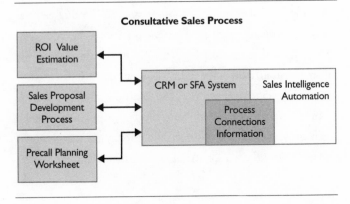

Figure 5.3 shows how an organization might store some of its process connections information in its CRM or SFA systems. Specifically, information is gathered during multiple phases of the sales process using tools such as a precall planning worksheet or ROI valuation tool. The information gathered is stored in the SFA system and used later for the sales proposal. A buyer's key pain points and their impact on the company are process connections information that is important to include in a sales intelligence system.

Process Connections Information Falls into Categories

We developed a list of the most commonly used and generic PCI categories and the associated sales phases in which

FIGURE 5.4 Where PCIs Originate

PCI CATEGORY	SALES PROCESS PHASE
Customer background information	Target, Qualify, Meet/Greet
Key issues, pains, and goals	Qualify, Meet/Greet
Impacts on business	Qualify, Meet/Greet, Presentation
Customer status quo	Meet/Greet, Presentation
Customer stated needs	Qualify, Meet/Greet, Presentation
Customer selection criteria	Qualify, Meet/Greet
Product/service application	Presentation, Proposal
Investment breakdown	Presentation, Proposal
Nonfinancial benefits	Presentation, Proposal
Financial benefits	Presentation, Proposal
Implementation/installation variables	Presentation, Proposal

they originate. Figure 5.4 also shows how PCIs can originate in more than one sales process phase.

Exercise: First Identify Your Process Connections Information Detail

Before you start listing your company's unique PCI categories, first identify the detail PCI you use. You can then use this knowledge to help you categorize it, as we'll show in later chapters. Use a table to identify some of the *detailed* PCI needed in your company's sales process.

Start with a blank sheet of paper and make three columns:

- Sales Process Phase
- Sales Activities
- Process Connections Information

Start by listing the first phase of your sales process. Next, list the activities that a sales professional completes during the phase. Finally, identify the specific process connections information required to complete each activity.

By completing this exercise, you will be building a foundation for further analysis of how PCI is gathered and used in your sales process. You will use the data entered in your table in subsequent chapters as a basis to help you understand and identify PCI gaps in your sales methodology, tools, and process. This represents knowledge most organizations need if they want to understand why their sales professionals aren't prepared to sell.

If, after completing this exercise, your table looks empty or the PCI detail is a bit sketchy, it might be symptomatic of the consultative sales methodology you are using (or, more likely, not using). You should at least be able to identify one or two sales activities per phase and the basic PCI detail that is gathered or used during each.

Stuff You Need to Remember

Common prospective customer information links sales phases and sales tools. We call this common customer information *process connections information (PCI)*.

- ✓ The PCI linkages between sales process phases enables and ensures a logical progression of prospect information–gathering throughout your sales process.
- ✓ In addition, the PCI linkages between sales tools assures needed prospect information is gathered and used at the appropriate time in the sales cycle and is available to be used later.
- ✓ When identifying gaps in your custom sales tool kit, you will need to understand what PCI links the sales tools to each other and consequently to the sales phase.
- ✓ Process connections information and prospective buyer information gathered throughout the sales process is used in many different ways by your organization. You use process connections information to
  - determine the quality of a lead,
  - reinforce and support the consultative sales process,
  - analyze and forecast sales,
  - establish a basis for recommending a solution,
  - assess the value you are capable of delivering, and
  - provide marketing with data for market analysis.

- ✓ Organizations must understand what and how PCI is gathered during its sales process to understand the gaps that must be filled.
- ✓ Customized sales tools help sales professionals gather and record PCI.

6

Two Flavors of Information— Sources and Uses

"We're in agreement then, nobody knows what the hell these statistics mean."

Johnny spent the next several weeks (in between sales calls) developing a series of sales tools, including: a precall planning worksheet, used to gather initial prospect information; a simple ROI questionnaire, used to identify issues, pains, and goals, and then assess value; and a basic proposal template, used to provide quotes and proposals. At some point, Johnny wants to develop a couple of phone message scripts, sponsor letters, and a competitive analysis database. His previous employer had provided these tools to Johnny as part of its sales training program. Johnny is frustrated to not have these basic elements in place, especially as he is facing many other challenges. He realizes the need to generate leads, nurture the corporate customer database, and at the same time build a set of best practices for the new sales force he someday hopes to hire. The tools he decides to create will help him to consistently capture relevant information to better qualify prospects, assess their current situation, and present a solution that will close more opportunities sooner. The issue, however, is simple: where is all the data and how does Johnny get it? In other words, the presales planning worksheet, ROI tool, and proposal template will only get him part of the data he will need to properly analyze, prescribe, and assist in the buying decision. Johnny needs to know more.

Now that we've explored process connections information (PCI), which we defined in the previous chapter as information about the prospect gathered at one phase (or phases) of the sales process and then used during another, it's time to take a look at the flavors of that information.

A sales professional doesn't passively accumulate PCI throughout the sales cycle. Rather, he or she *gathers* PCI as the result of proactive and consultative activities. The ways a salesperson gathers PCI include:

- Performing a search in one of the online corporate information business databases, like Harris Infosearch, Jigsaw, or Sales Genie, to gather some information needed to complete a custom precall planning worksheet to prepare for the first call to a prospect or target.
- If the prospect is a publicly held company, its annual report, 10K, and any SEC filings will be available on its Web site. These documents explain a lot about a company's strategy and direction.
- Performing a Web site search to learn about the prospect's company, products, customer base, and so on.
- Completing prospect and ROI questionnaires to further understand the prospect's unique situation, key challenges, and needs.

A sales professional also uses PCI throughout the sales cycle. A sales professional might use it to

- determine the customer's system configuration requirements to price a system,

- develop an ROI valuation to prove the proposed product or service's value proposition,
- write a confirmation letter to confirm the prospect's needs, and/or
- write a sales proposal to provide the prospect's decision makers with information on which they can base an informed buying decision.

To work effectively and efficiently as a consultative sales professional, you must systematically gather *and* use PCI throughout your sales process. Of course, it's very important to know when to gather the needed PCI and how to make proper use of it once gathered. Customized sales tools make this possible.

Do Your Homework

At ROI4Sales, we use a precall planning worksheet that we custom-designed to prepare us for the first call to a new prospect or target. We first perform a search using Harris Infosearch to gather some basic information, such as company size, executive contacts, and annual revenue. Harris Infosearch is a Dun & Bradstreet research service that provides information about any company and its subsidiaries. Next, we perform a Web site search to understand the company's products, services, and general audience (or customer base), and to determine just how savvy the company is in regards to using value estimation in its marketing program. Finally, we review our objectives for the call and decide what questions will need answers based on the data we have already collected. We document each bit of data in our SFA system and use it on the initial call, follow-up confirmation letter, and throughout the sales process. We collect data early in the sales process to qualify a prospect and use it again later to help us calculate the potential value we can deliver later. Finally, as part of our sales process, we use our own ROI model to estimate the return on investment we can deliver to our prospects.

Homework Pays Off

One of the key pains we address is to help organizations reduce their discounting. In Figure 6.1 we use the revenue figure captured earlier in the sales process to help us calculate the annual loss from discounting. Notice how we only needed to ask one more question once we learned annual revenue to estimate a value we are capable of delivering. Remember, do your research up front, and you will only need to confirm what you already know.

As you can see from the example, this is a $27 million company that discounts, on average, 20 percent annually. The discount is costing it $6.75 million a year.

We collect data throughout the sales process and use the data to generate output that assists the buyer in making an informed decision.

FIGURE 6.1 Increase Revenue with a Reduction in Discounting

ROI selling will help reduce or eliminate discounting due to our robust Financial Dashboard and the ability to display the value delivered. There are several calculations that indicate Net Present Value (NPV) or investment and Internal Rate of Return (IRR) as well as a section on the cost of status quo and the cost of delay in the purchase.

Enter your average discount rate on your products and services:	20%
Annual (direct sales) revenue: (From General Information)	$27,000,000
Calculated revenue lost due to discounting:	$6,750,000

A typical ROI Selling customer reduces discounting by up to 50%

Arena Software has virtually eliminated discounting, and increased prices as a result of ROI Selling

Enter the reduction in discounting from utilizing ROI Selling:	5%
Estimated revenue recaptured from reducing discounting:	**$337,500**

Sales Tools in the Sales Process Force Behavior Patterns

We define sales tools as follows:

A *sales tool* is any document, form, or system that: 1) directly supports a company's sales professionals in following its consultative sales methodology, and 2) provides the prospective customer with information on which to make an informed buying decision.

Sales tools are integral to the sales process itself. They represent a critical link between what your company sells and how it sells it. Why is this important? Because sales tools force sales professionals to gather, process, and disseminate vital process connections information at certain points in the sales process. If your sales professionals aren't using some of your sales tools, they're probably not following much of your sales process either.

Organizations must provide their sales force with custom sales tools designed specifically to sell their products and services. Each sales tool must be integrated with the other sales tools, the sales methodology, and the sales process phases or steps. Obviously, you can't just give the sales force a pile of custom sales tools and expect them to start using them. We strongly recommend custom training programs that incorporate the use of custom sales tools as part of your corporate commitment to a consultative sales program.

Here's what to expect if your organization doesn't provide its sales force with the custom sales tools and training:

- Salespeople will be forced to develop their own sales tools apart from corporate culture and without input or control—seems a bit implausible and/or just scary.
- The company will lose control over the integrity of its corporate image and brand—just read a sales proposal written by one of the new guys if you don't believe this.

- Silos (independent pods) of information will be created throughout the sales and potentially the marketing organizations—you might begin to fix this with a CRM implementation.
- Salespeople will skip over required phases or steps in the sales process, likely lowering close ratios—perhaps closer to reality.

Sales management will lose the opportunity to track success or failure in the postsale (or loss) review—How many proposals did your company write last year? What's your *Proposal Close Ratio?*

Customization Gets You Extra Credit (and Probably More Revenue)

When a company develops custom sales tools for its sales professionals, it simultaneously bridges the gap between its consultative sales process and product or service training. To effectively customize a sales tool, you must first understand the purpose of the tool.

For example, a precall planning worksheet is typically used to gather prospective customer information prior to the first call. It must include whether or not a prospect is capable of purchasing your products and services. Before reading further, complete this exercise. Begin by defining and documenting your "perfect" size prospect and work backward to the minimum requirements—this is PCI detail.

Once you have defined the minimum requirements, develop questions to determine whether or not a prospect has the motive and a means for purchasing from you.

This exercise can be used for each of your sales tools. When using an ROI tool, for example, you must ask questions that will identify the current cost of pain your organization can resolve. It serves no purpose to ask questions about issues, pains, or goals you can't address.

Don't forget to add your logo to all your documents and use your vernacular throughout. You wouldn't believe how many "custom" tools we see where the company doesn't add its logo or use its unique terminology to describe the information requirements it has.

Often the buyer information requirements of the custom sales tools compel salespeople to learn enough about the buyer's operation to define clearly the application of the proposed product or service in the buyer's business. This typically helps the salesperson to describe its value proposition.

Here are some basic sales tools we recommend to our customers:

- Sales intelligence systems—to capture and store sales-related data to be used later for sophisticated searches
- Confirmation letters—to confirm prospect issues, pains, and goals
- Precall planning worksheet—to gather basic prospect information prior to the first call

- ROI questionnaire—to identify issues, pains, and goals, and establish the cost of status quo
- Pricing/configuration system—to determine correct system configuration prior to close
- ROI valuation—to summarize questionnaire data and prove value to be delivered
- Sales proposal—to present understanding of prospect, proposed solution, implementation, and seller information
- 360-degree ROI—to measure value delivered 12 to 18 months after implementation
- CRM/SFA—to collect and store PCI on prospects and customers

Please see the Resources section in the back of the book for a more complete list of sales tools and vendors who market them.

Sales Tools: Sources or Uses?

eGistics Inc., one of our clients, uses an ROI questionnaire we built for it throughout its sales process. It requires sales professionals to identify the prospect's key pain indicators. A key pain indicator question is a question asked by the sales professional to identify an issue, pain, or goal a prospect has that eGistics knows it can resolve. eGistics's ROI questionnaire represents a sales tool for gathering specific process connections information, and it becomes a *source* of PCI after a sales professional completes it. Later in the sales cycle, the sales professional might *use* the key pain indicators from the questionnaire in a letter to confirm the validity of the problem with the prospect. eGistics's confirmation letter is a standard sales process letter, a custom sales tool that *uses* process connections information from the ROI questionnaire. An eGistics sales professional might also present the findings of the ROI valuation (more PCI) in a sales proposal and supporting presentation (Microsoft Power-Point, for example). These represent sales process deliverables, which are also sales tools, from the presentation phase. They represent some eGistics sales tools that *use* the same PCI as the confirmation letter—the key pain indicators from the ROI questionnaire.

Figure 6.2 illustrates how the eGistics ROI questionnaire is a *source* of PCI, the key pain indicators that its sales professionals later *use* to write confirmation letters and sales proposals and develop supporting presentations.

Gather Up Your Sales Tools

Create another three-column table. Label the columns Sales Tools, Process Connections Information Categories, and Source/Use/Both. List each of the custom sales tools you have available for your sales force. Remember to include letter templates, proposal templates, a CRM, and/or an SFA

FIGURE 6.2 Uses of Questionnaire

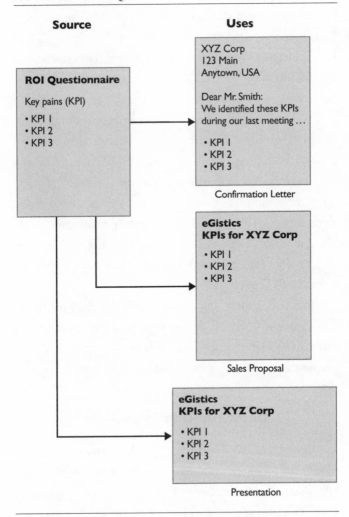

Stupid Is As Stupid Does

While Johnny was developing his own sales tools, it became evident that he needed to collect specific information at certain points in the sales process. One of Johnny's problems was that his precall planning worksheet didn't integrate with his ROI questionnaire or the SFA system corporate forced him to use. Therefore, he wasn't always sure whether he had collected the right information from a prospect unless he went back and looked at each sales tool and compared their content.

Because of this lack of integration, Johnny often collected the same information from a prospect multiple times. Johnny needed to ensure his sales tools were fully integrated and collected all the appropriate PCI throughout the sales process.

system. For each sales tool, define the major category or categories of process connections information each contains. Use the last column to define the sales tool's relationship to PCI; enter *source, use,* or *both.*

For Johnny and other selling organizations, the term *integration* takes on two meanings. First, it can mean the physical integration of sales tools. For example, programming a configuration tool into an SFA system, so sales professionals are able to automatically send the sales proposal system the appropriate information from their desktop SFA system. Second, it can mean simply gathering PCI in one sales tool to use it in another without necessarily being physically connected (manually reentering the information when necessary). We strongly advise physical (automated) integration as much as possible; yet we realize this may be beyond your company's capability and capacity. Nonphysical integration, entering and reentering data into multiple systems and sales tools, is a necessity for a consultative selling process to succeed. Though it feels like a great waste of time to reenter the same information multiple times, not doing so will make anyone look stupid if they keep asking the same questions from the earliest stages of the sales process.

Self-Assessment

Take a moment and assess your current situation as it pertains to your company's sales tools. In Figure 6.3, the horizontal axis indicates the level of customization for your current sales tools. Rate your company on a scale of 1–4. Be sure to include in your analysis: letter templates, ROI tools, proposals, sales intelligence systems, CRM or SFA systems, and so on. The vertical axis dictates the commitment of your management team to the customization of your sales tools. Commitment includes financing the customization, building automated integration, maintenance, and development

FIGURE 6.3 Sales Tools Assessment Chart

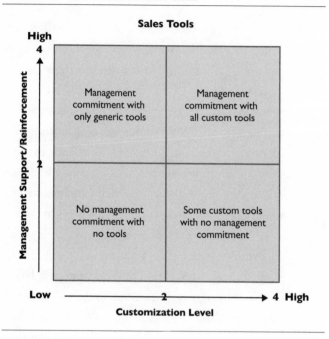

of new tools. The combination is what we are interested in at this point. For example, if you currently use a generic sales methodology, custom survey, generic ROI tool, generic sales letters, and a semicustom proposal template with no standard training, and little or no budget for updating and maintaining the tools, you would likely fall into the lower left quadrant. Add these ratings together. The higher your organization rates on the scale, the better your opportunity for success in sales.

Score Analysis

- **0:** Your organization lacks adequate sales tool customization and the management commitment to be successful at consultative selling—no tools and no process is not a good way to go through life.

- **1–2:** Although you are making strides in either acquiring management commitment or customizing your sales tools, there is still a major lack of both to make much of an impact on the sales process. Either you have only a few tools or little management commitment to get some. Both situations are problematic.

- **3–4:** You have gained momentum and have an opportunity to succeed. However, watch out for creating silos of information and nonintegrated sales tools within your company. You must have management commitment to back your sales tools development. Pull it all together and identify what you need to create a complete integrated program.

- **5–6:** You are on your way to a very successful career, but you may have a lot of sales tool customization to do to be successful. Identify the missing pieces and budget for integration into your sales process.

- **7–8:** Excellent job! You are on you way to a very successful sales career. Remember, having management commitment and lots of custom sales tools is only part of the mix; you still need to execute.

In the next chapter, we discuss the need to know what process connections information is required at what phase in the sales process. To help you understand this better, we will give you an exercise in which you will define your sales tools and identify them as sources or uses of PCI. Finally, we discuss the need to control the sales process, as opposed to controlling the sale.

Stuff You Need to Remember

A company's customized sales tools represent its unique *sources* and *uses* of process connections information, the prospect information that its sales professionals need to sell its products or services. To be effective, a selling organization must customize its sales tools to match its specific products or services and fit them within the framework of the consultative sales methodology it uses. If a company doesn't provide its sales professionals with sales tools

- it forces them to create their own (unlikely);
- they may skip critical sales process activities (likely); or
- it may create an environment with silos of information (pre-CRM or SFA reality).

There are many commercially available sales tools that a company can acquire and customize to help sales professionals collect PCI that will also fill in the gaps between sales methodology training and product training; they include:

- ROI questionnaires
- Business development and confirmation letters
- Sales intelligence systems
- Automated sales proposal production systems
- CRM/SFA systems
- Price and product configuration systems

Integration of custom sales tools is important to a company's commitment. Keep in mind:

✓ Physical integration (or automation) is important but not required.
✓ Nonautomated integration is required to succeed at a consultative sales process; although collecting process connections in a nonautomated environment is time-consuming and error-prone.

7

Sales Tools in the Sales Process

SALES PROCESS

"Everybody's specializing these days."

With the custom sales tools he himself developed (a precall planning worksheet, ROI questionnaire, and a custom proposal), Johnny felt more confident in his product's capabilities and his ability to sell. Although these sales tools were the basics and a good start, Johnny still felt he wasn't making enough progress in building a foundation for the staff he would eventually hire.

His idea was simple: Johnny wanted to create a standard set of sales tools that would capture information, assess value, and present solutions, and then package them to use in a successful, repeatable sales process. Johnny enlisted the help and guidance of Sara, the corporate marketing director, to help design, build, and provide ongoing support for the new sales tool kit. Dave had assured Johnny he would have marketing's support from day one, but even after several months, Johnny had yet to see that put into practice.

Making More of the Connections

We have discussed the concept that sales tools can be both *sources* and *uses* of information at various phases of the sales process. We have also emphasized the importance of knowing whether a sales tool is a source, a use, or both a source and use of PCI. Knowing this about PCI is important for two reasons. *First,* by documenting your sales tools as sources and uses, you can easily identify gaps in the information-gathering activities of your sales process (and avoid looking stupid). You must understand what information you need, where it comes from, and when you should ask for it. *Second,* with an understanding of what PCI resides within each sales tool, you can determine where information is held so it can be used by other sales tools. For example, the buyer's critical business issues are used in a confirmation letter and a sales proposal. This knowledge of PCI will keep you from duplicating efforts as you create or enhance your new sales tool kit.

When ROI4Sales began building tools for our sales force, we started with our ROI-on-ROI model—a custom sales tool for what we sell, not some generic ROI-on-Widgets model. This model captured primary issues, pains, and goals, and the current cost of the status quo, and quantified the value we could deliver. The problem was that it didn't capture other basic PCI on the prospect, such as how it tracks revenue, is it a division or subsidiary of a larger organization, its revenue breakdown by services, existing customers, or new business. In other words, the ROI-on-ROI does not capture non-ROI information.

Our first inclination was to add it to our model. After all, it seemed logical to capture all PCI in one sales tool. This, however, would have been a mistake because it would have diluted the value and impact of our custom ROI-on-ROI tool in the sales process. We decided to create a sales process survey to use after the custom precall planning worksheet was completed. This would accept the information already collected from the worksheet sheet, ask the additional questions we needed for our consultative sales approach, and then send ROI data to the ROI questionnaire.

Sounds like some of that integration stuff is taking place, doesn't it? As a result, our sales force didn't have to re-ask and reenter the prospect's responses, thus increasing productivity.

Notice the data in Figure 7.1 is used in the prospect questionnaire and then also in the ROI model. Rather than force the precall sheet to become the prospect questionnaire and the prospect questionnaire to become the ROI model, we created and customized tools that serve a particular purpose, and used the PCI in one tool for use in other tools with a specific purpose. The PCI from all three tools will be used to create sales process letters and a sales proposal (see Figure 7.2).

FIGURE 7.1 Where Data Is Used

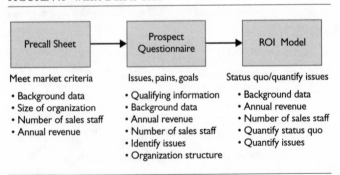

Precall Sheet	Prospect Questionnaire	ROI Model
Meet market criteria	Issues, pains, goals	Status quo/quantify issues
• Background data	• Qualifying information	• Background data
• Size of organization	• Background data	• Annual revenue
• Number of sales staff	• Annual revenue	• Number of sales staff
• Annual revenue	• Number of sales staff	• Quantify status quo
	• Identify issues	• Quantify issues
	• Organization structure	

FIGURE 7.2 Flow of PCI through Tools

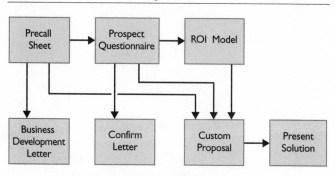

Breaking Down Your Sales Phases

Figure 7.3 is based on the eight-phase sales process we introduced in Chapter 5. It displays several sales tools sorted by the phase in which they are primarily used. Then we added whether the tool is a source, use, or both of process connections information. Take a moment to review the different sources and uses of information as it flows from one sales phase into the next.

Sales Tools Reinforce Consultative Selling

An additional benefit of customizing your sales tools is the ability to determine what your sales professionals must do to complete a sequence of specific sales activities. If a sales tool is designed for a specific purpose (like an ROI tool, for example), as a *source* or *use* of process connections

FIGURE 7.3 Sales Tools Sorted by Sales Process Phase

SALES PHASE	SALES TOOL: PURPOSE	PROCESS CONNECTIONS INFORMATION	SOURCE/USE
Target	**Sales intelligence system:** Performs sophisticated searches for sales-related data	Repository for sales process information, research, templates, etc.	Both
	Business development letter: Initial contact and introduction to prospect	Initial prospect data, confirmation of ability to meet marketing criteria	Use
Qualify	**Prospect survey:** Helps gather and process prospect information	Prospect data, initial qualifying information, decision process, team structure, stated goals and needs next steps, company background	Source
	ROI key pain indicator (KPI) input questionnaire: Helps identify issues, pains, and goals and calculates current cost of status quo	Issues, pains, and goals—data for calculating current cost of status quo	Both
	Confirmation letter: Confirms prospect information and/or key pains and current cost of status quo	Prospect background, confirms issues, pains, and goals, and calculates current cost of status quo	Use

FIGURE 7.3 Sales Tools Sorted by Sales Process Phase (*Continued*)

Meet/Greet	**ROI questionnaire:** Confirms issues, pains, and goals, identifies current cost of status quo, estimates value proposition	Issues, pains, and goals, current cost of status quo, value proposition	Both
	Confirmation letter (2): Confirms key issues, pains, and goals, confirm s current cost of status quo, discusses value proposition	Issues, pains, and goals, impact on business, current cost of status quo	Use
Presentation	**ROI questionnaire:** Confirms issues, confirms current cost, estimates value, proves value proposition	Issues, pains, goals, current cost of status quo, prospect specific value deliverables, value proposition proven	Both
	Confirmation letter (3): Confirms value proposition, preliminary solution, and investment	Preliminary investment (cost), product or service configuration, and value estimation	Both
Proposal	**Pricing/Configuration system:** Configures proposed solution and applies cost analysis	Prospect information, proposed solution, investment breakdown	Both
	Sales proposal: Finally confirms issues, pains, and goals and current state of affairs, educates the buyer on services and options, provides ROI model and investment breakdown	Issues, pains, and goals, current cost of status quo, value estimation, ROI, configuration, and investment breakdown	Use

FIGURE 7.3 Sales Tools Sorted by Sales Process Phase *(Continued)*

Proposal (cont.)	**Presentation:** Presents proposal to prospect's decision makers	Issues, pains, and goals, current cost of status quo, configuration, investment breakdown	Use
	Transmittal letter: Is cover letter to sales proposal	Issues, pains, and goals, current cost of status quo, configuration, investment breakdown	Use
Due Diligence	**Case studies:** Provides prospect with examples of similar product or service applications	Current and past prospect successes	Use
	Prospect testimonials: Provides prospect with references	Current prospect experiences	Use
Close	**Closed sale checklist:** Ensures all sales process activities, deliverables, and other documents have been completed	List of sales tools completed for a prospect	Use
Postsales	**360° ROI assessment:** Evaluates actual ROI valuation results after implementation	Previous and current key pains and other prospect information	Both
	Win-loss analysis: Debriefs and analyzes sale	Reasons for win or loss, prospect's selection criteria	Both

information, then the component's purpose also defines its related sales process activity. For example, AQS Software requires its sales professionals to write a letter following the presentation phase confirming the proposed configuration before proceeding (see Figure 7.4). The letter is a sales tool and *use* of PCI. The PCI requirements of the letter mean the salesperson must use the company's configuration tool first, which is the process connections *source* of the configuration information. In this way, the letter is a sales process activity that must occur at a specific point in the sales process. It's also a deliverable—the prospect receives it at a defined point and, ideally, it moves the prospect along in the process. Obviously, AQS custom sales tools reinforce and help control their consultative sales process.

FIGURE 7.4 Custom Sales Tools Facilitating the Sales Process

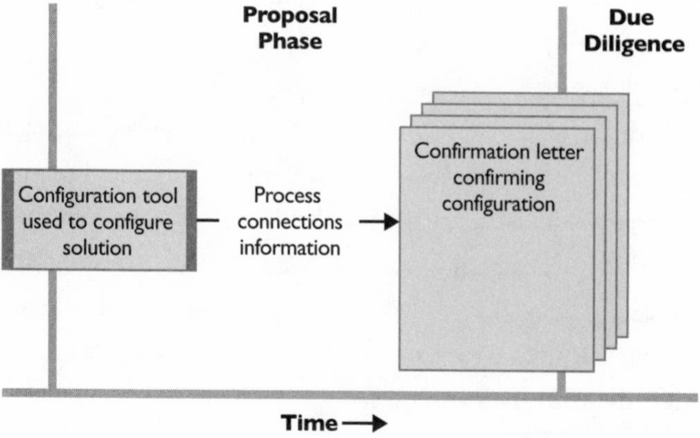

If a company can determine what PCI it needs to sell its products and services and how it wants to use that information, it can define the sales process activities related to its sales tools. This concept is important to help you control the flow of a sale. Remember, though you likely can't control the sale, you can control the process. Having a custom, defined sales process with supporting sales tools is particularly advantageous when forecasting revenue and, of course, training new personnel.

Build It and They May Come
(Or Somebody Might Buy from You)

In Chapter 5 we directed you to develop and document your sales process phases, and in Chapter 6 we guided you through documenting your current sales tools. Now, add to this data, this time entering the PCI category you are collecting and selecting whether your tool is a source, a use, or both.

In the next chapter, we discuss negotiating value at each phase of the sales process to capture the PCI required to provide your prospects with what they need to make informed decisions—ideally in your favor. We also discuss when in the process you need to collect certain information. Finally, we provide templates to map your PCI to your sales process and identify its sources and uses.

Stuff You Need to Remember

A company's custom sales tools represent the *sources* and *uses* of process connections information at various stages of the sales process. When following a consultative sales approach, it is crucial to understand what PCI is needed at what point in the process. You also need to understand what sales tools are capable of capturing the information required.

- ✓ Build your custom sales tool kit based on the PCI you will need to assess the current situation, prescribe a plan of action, and recommend a solution to the critical issues, pains, and goals.
- ✓ Use custom sales tools for the purpose they were designed: to collect or use the PCI needed to reinforce related consultative selling activities with your salespeople.
- ✓ Use the deliverables your sales professionals give to your prospects, some very important uses of PCI, to help you control the sales process.

8

Making the Connection

"Brewster, I think it's time we had a chat about your priorities."

Johnny, Dave, and Sara met at the beginning of the quarter to discuss the sales tools and resources Johnny felt he needed to be successful. Johnny showed off his templates, demonstrating how the prospect questionnaire, precall planning worksheet, ROI questionnaire, and sales proposal all had varying degrees of success throughout the sales process. He discussed how the standard methodology corporate had forced upon him needed to be customized and integrated with the tools he had developed to create a successful, repeatable sales process. Johnny also wanted to add several tools to his sales tool kit.

Dave pointed out the current lack of budget for sales tool development. Sara pointed out that many of the tools Johnny wanted already existed within the corporation; all Johnny needed to do was find and update them. Neither saw Johnny's needs as terribly pressing. Feeling frustrated, Johnny blurted out, "I'm so sick of this 'If it ain't broke, don't fix it' attitude. It's obviously broken, and all the rest is just excuses! Hope is not a strategy!"

While Johnny knew he didn't win anyone over with his temper tantrum, or homage to Rick Page (author of Hope Is Not a Strategy), *the fact was, Johnny wanted more. He wanted his company to support him with resources that would ensure his success selling their products and services.*

Up to this point, you've assessed your current situation as it pertains to sales tools, processes, and the information connections between them. In the previous three chapters, we

- introduced consultative selling through a customized sales methodology;
- discussed process connections information, which is prospect information gathered during a sales process phase and used during another;
- showed you how your PCI is directly related to custom sales tools and utilized throughout the sales process; and
- guided you through developing a PCI source-and-use table.

You can make your sales process airtight by using your sources and uses of PCI to determine gaps in your existing sales process and tools. We start by using five basic sales tools and identifying what we believe to be typical and primary categories of PCI.

Process Connections Mapping— An Example

It should be easy to see the connections between the following five basic sales tools and understand their interdependencies. You can see in Figure 8.1 the common PCI listed in these five sales tools.

- The prospect survey and ROI valuation tools are *sources* of PCI.

FIGURE 8.1   Common PCI in Five Basic Sales Tools

SALES TOOL	PURPOSE	PCI CATEGORIES
Prospect sales survey	Capture and process prospect information during the sales process	• Background information • Key pains • Stated needs and goals • Selection criteria • Implementation/ Installation variables
KPI input questionnaire	Capture key issues, pains, and goals, and establish current cost of status quo	• Key pain indicators • Current cost of status quo
ROI valuation tool	Develop a custom ROI valuation for the prospect	• Key issues, pains, and goals • Impacts on business • Current cost of status quo • Potential financial benefits
Sales process letter	Confirm ROI valuation results	• Key pain indicators (select) • Product/service application (overview) • Investment (preliminary) • Potential financial benefits

FIGURE 8.1 Common PCI in Five Basic Sales Tools *(Continued)*

SALES TOOL	PURPOSE	PCI CATEGORIES
Sales proposal	Present results of sales process to buyer's decision makers	• Background information • Key issues, pains, and goals • Impacts on business • Prospect needs • Product/Service application • Investment breakdown • Financial benefits • Nonfinancial benefits • Implementation/ Installation variables

- The ROI valuation tool *uses* PCI from the KPI input questionnaire and its output is a deliverable.
- The letter and proposal are deliverables to the prospective buyer and represent *uses* of PCI from the survey, KPI input, and ROI valuation tool.

Figure 8.2 makes it easier to see the relation between the five basic sales tools and the primary process connections categories we believe are critical for many sales tools to contain. These primary categories can be used as a foundation for information requirements in most consultative sales environments. Remember, these are only guidelines and must

FIGURE 8.2 Source/Use Table

PROCESS CONNECTIONS INFORMATION

SALES TOOLS	Background Information	Critical Issues	Impacts on Business	Stated Needs	Customer's Selection Criteria	Product Application	Investment Breakdown	Nonfinancial Benefits	Financial Benefits	Implementation Variables
Prospect Survey	S	S		S	S					
KPI Input	U	S		S						
ROI Valuation	U	S	S	S		U	U		S	
Sales Process Letter (confirm ROI valuation)	U	U	U	U		U	U	S	U	
Sales Proposal	U	U	U	U	U	U	U	U	U	U

be customized for your company. How many of these primary PCI categories are used in your sales process?

As you would expect, each column should contain at least one *source* and one *use* of the required PCI. Using the table begins to identify the interrelationships and interdependencies of the custom sales tools. If a column does not contain at least one source (S) and one use (U), a gap exists and must be resolved before moving forward. In Chapter 9, we'll discuss how to fill in these gaps.

Note that three of the five sales tools listed "use" in the product/service application and investment breakdown categories, but there is no source for the information. This implies there is a sales tool or tools missing that needs to supply the source for the tools listed as uses of that information. The implementation/installation variables category also has no source identified. These gaps might occur when you are preparing a proposal, for example, when information is not available to complete the sales proposal, and the salesperson is forced to improvise. How often does this happen in your organization? What is the impact or liability to your organization each time this occurs?

Mapping Process Connections, Sales Tools, and Sales Cycle Phases

Knowing when a sales tool is used during the sales process helps to define the sales activities needed to support it, and to understand when these sales activities should occur.

Now is the time to add a time dimension to the eight-phase sales methodology table that was started in Chapter 5 (see Figure 8.3). This will show the sales process phase or phases in which each category of PCI is gathered or used and which sales tools are involved. Notice that during the qualify, meet/greet, and presentation phases, the salesperson must gather, process, or define the PCI in more than half of the categories. Is this the same for your sales process?

FIGURE 8.3   Sales Process Phases Where PCI Is Gathered

SALES TOOLS	PROCESS CONNECTIONS INFORMATION										SALES PROCESS PHASES							
	Background Information	Key Issues	Impacts on Business	Customer's Stated Needs	Customer's Selection Criteria	Product Application	Investment Breakdown	Nonfinancial Benefits	Financial Benefits	Implementation Variables	Target	Qualify	Meet/Greet	Presentation	Proposal	Due Diligence	Close	Postsales
Prospect Survey	S	S		S	S							X	X	X	X			
KPI Input	U	S		S								X	X	X				
ROI Valuation	U	S	S	S		U	U		S					X	X	X	X	X
Sales Process Letter (confirm ROI valuation)	U	U	U	U		U	U	S	U				X		X			
Sales Proposal	U	U	U	U	U	U	U	U	U	U					X	X	X	

Most consultative sales processes require sales professionals to gather and digest lots of buyer information during the early phases. Obviously, it's critical that this information is available for the other sales tools to use in later phases. Note the dependencies that are taking place. For example, you can't write a sales proposal until you have completed the ROI valuation. A sales professional can't write a proposal until he or she meets the PCI requirements of all the categories.

The example in Figure 8.3 illustrates a very simple approach to mapping your sales tools to your sales process and identifying any corresponding gaps. We strongly recommend that you make your own table like the one in this figure. Here are are a few things to keep in mind as you do so:

Identify all of your sales tools in the center column, being sure to include standard tools, such as ROI tools, sales process letters, and CRM and/or SFA systems. Then enter the primary categories of PCI from our examples, or create your own. After entering your sales process phases, determine the sales process phase or phases in which each sales tool is used or produced by placing an "X" in each of the appropriate phase columns. Then enter an "S" for source, a "U" for use, a "B" for both, and finally an "R" for a repository of data.

Self-Assessment

Take a moment and assess your current situation as it pertains to sales tool integration within your sales process.

FIGURE 8.4 Sales Process Integration Assessment Chart

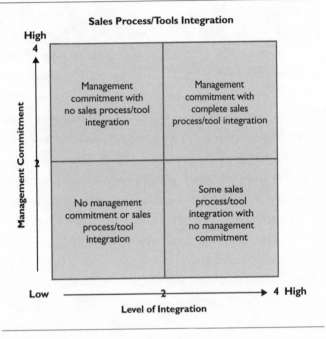

In Figure 8.4, the horizontal axis indicates your level of integration for your current sales tools. Do you have tools that are tasked to be completed at various phases of your sales process? For example, do you have process letters that must be sent after completing a prospect questionnaire? Or do you complete ROI questionnaires only after a prospect meets certain criteria and has signed off on the issues, pains, and goals defined earlier in the process?

The vertical axis indicates the commitment of your management team to the integration of your sales tools into your sales process, including financing the systems and the physical integration of tools into your process. Rate your level of integration on a scale of 1 to 4. For example, is the production of your sales proposal transmittal letters automated? Do you have an automated proposal production system? Rate your management commitment on a scale of 1 to 4. Add these ratings together. The combination of process integration and management commitment is what we are interested in at this point. If you currently use a generic spreadsheet ROI model and have no integration from a questionnaire or proposal, then you would likely fall into the box labeled no management commitment or sales process integration. Add these ratings together. The higher your score, the better equipped you are for sales success.

Score Analysis

- **0:** Your organization lacks adequate sales tool integration and management commitment to really be successful at consultative selling.
- **1–2:** Although you are making strides in either management support and commitment or integration of custom sales tools into the sales process, there is still a major lack of both to make much of an impact on the sales process.

- **3–4:** You have gained momentum in either integration or management commitment and have an opportunity to succeed. Pull it all together and identify what you need to create a complete integrated program, either additional integration or increased management commitment.

- **5–6:** You are on your way to very successful results but you need more management commitment. You still have a lot of integration work to do to be successful, but you should have management support to get it done.

- **7–8:** Excellent job! You should be experiencing some good sales successes. Remember, though, this is only one component to success.

In the next chapter we have you take a look at the gaps that may exist in your current sales materials and customized sales tools. We make a comparison to the time, effort, and resources used to develop your corporate Web site. We also provide a series of questions that will help you analyze the gaps that may need your attention. Finally, we discuss the need for an entity within your corporation to take ownership of the design, build, and deployment of each of the customized sales tools.

Stuff You Need to Remember

Remember, you must negotiate the exchange of information in each interaction with your prospect. It is crucial that you understand what information is required to help you close the opportunity and that you provide your prospects with what he or she needs to make informed buying decisions. It's also important that you know in what sales process phase you should ask for specific information and where it needs to reside because it will help you design, develop, and integrate custom sales tools.

✓ You must have a source for every PCI use.
✓ Use tools for what they were designed to do.
✓ Identify gaps by mapping interdependencies of sales process phases, sales tools, and process connections information.

9

Gaps Are Bad

"No, Harris, you can't take sick leave just because you don't feel positive today."

After the frustrating meeting with his boss and marketing, Johnny wanted to quit and go back to his old job where he had sales resources and custom sales tools given to him. He couldn't understand why there was so much reluctance to invest in the tools necessary to succeed. After all, this company had invested hundreds of thousands of dollars into spinning off this organization but was refusing to put budgeted dollars into the most fundamental revenue-generating asset they had: Johnny. In his past company, he had strong management commitment in all these areas.

Deciding to push the envelope a bit, he gift-wrapped two copies of Rick Page's book Hope Is Not a Strategy, *one for Dave and one for Sara. On each copy, he flagged the following passage: "New models of selling demand new skill sets, better understanding of the client's business, and the ability to work collaboratively to solve business problems rather than to sell products."*

Determined not to complain any longer but to keep after them and demand change, Johnny decided it was time to provide them with a gap list. This list would have to be created without emotion, just listing the facts. Johnny would analyze what sales tools he had available to him, rating them in terms of usefulness and potential for improvement in his newly devised sales process.

In preparation to analyze the gaps in your sales process, methodology, and tools, you will need to refer back to the chart you've been developing. In Chapter 8, you identified

> *Selling Power Magazine* conducted a survey on why salespeople fail and concluded that about 25 percent of them fail from "poor attitude." How many players on your team have a poor attitude?

PCI sources (S) and uses (U) and, based on that, determined where gaps existed. To identify the gaps effectively, though, you must look deeper into what you have and what is missing. In this chapter, we guide you through this analysis process and help you identify gaps in methodology, tools, and process. Let's begin with some basic questions you need to answer as part of the analysis process:

- Can your sales force clearly define the phases of your sales process and the purpose of each?
- Can your sales force identify the sales tools and resources available to them at each phase of your sales process?
- Has your company invested in a sales methodology? If yes, have you hired outside sources to customize its deployment?
- Is there an individual or department responsible for maintaining each of your sales tools?
- Do the sales and marketing organizations work together on branding and messaging?

According to a *Selling Power Magazine* survey, 56 percent of people surveyed are not satisfied with the technology solutions implemented in the past 12 months to enhance the sales process.

If you answered no to any of these questions, you probably have some gaps in your sales methodology, process, or tools. You will soon see how many and how big they are.

Identify the Tool and Deliverable (aka Where's the Hole?)

Create and complete a table like the example in Figure 9.1 with all your company's sales tools, including the sales process deliverables that you now have or feel you need for your salespeople. Be sure to include the various questionnaires your sales force uses to collect information, marketing CDs, letter models or templates, brochures, white papers or research documents you offer as incentives to contact your organization, or anything else a salesperson uses or gives to a prospect during the sales cycle. Figure 9.1 includes a coding structure to simplify your entries and help you assess your current situation.

FIGURE 9.1 Sales Tools Chart

SALES PHASE	SALES TOOL	T/D	AVAILABLE	CUSTOM	PURPOSE	OWNERSHIP RESPONSIBILITY
Proposal	Sales Proposal	D	Y	Y	Formal proposal to prospect	Sales, Marketing, Product Mgmt, and Professional Services
	Transmittal Letter	D		Y	Custom letter to prospect contact used as a cover letter for sales proposal	Sales

COLUMN	COMMENTS/DIRECTIONS
Sales Phase	Sales phase name. List phases in sequence.
Sales Tool	The name of the sales tool, deliverable, system, etc.
T/D	T = Tool; D = Deliverable
Available	Y = Yes currently available; Blank = not currently available
Custom	Y = Yes, the tool is or needs to be customized for our company; Blank = not customized
Purpose	Briefly define the purpose of each tool.
Ownership Responsibility	Identify what department or individual is responsible for the design and development of the tool or deliverable; however, if ownership responsibility doesn't exist, leave this cell blank. Keep in mind, if ownership responsibility currently doesn't exist, this represents a gap. Note: Sales professionals should not be responsible for the design or development of these tools or deliverables; they only should be responsible for correctly using them.

Reality Check

Before analyzing your own results, why not validate reality. Distribute a blank version of this table that you created to your sales force or select members of your sales force and ask them to complete it. If your sales professionals really follow and understand how to use the sales tools in your company's consultative sales methodology, they should be able to easily complete all the columns, except perhaps the ownership responsibility column—they may not know who is responsible for maintaining each tool. If they can't complete this table, then you have sales methodology training, implementation, and management problems.

Once you have completed the table, you're ready to identify the sales tool and deliverable gaps in your consultative selling methodology. Start by answering these questions:

- How many sales tools have you identified as needed but are not available?
- Which sales tools, including process deliverables, does your company need to develop?
- How many sales tools and deliverables are available but not customized?
- Which tools and deliverables does your company now have but need to be customized?
- How many sales tools and deliverables have no assigned responsibility?

- Which sales tools and deliverables have no assigned responsibility?

Each of these questions will help you hone in on the gaps in your sales methodology, process, and tools your organization is facing. We are going to state the obvious, but if the questions have long answers you have some issues that need to be addressed sooner rather than later. First you need to identify which sales tools are needed. Remember we asked you to enter into the charts even the tools you feel you need but don't have. Next, determine which sales tools you currently have available but need to be customized. Finally, it is essential to evaluate the ownership of each sales tool.

Someone Please Take Ownership

To deploy successfully a fully customized and integrated sales methodology, you need someone to take ownership for its development and maintenance. For example, organizations will assign a system administrator for their SFA or accounting systems but will fail to assign responsibility for their sales methodology and all its tools. Who's responsible for designing and maintaining business development letters in your company? Who's responsible for ensuring your proposal models contain the most current product and service information? Or sales materials, ROI tools, pricing or configuration information? Don't say your sales professionals have this responsibility. Your individual salespeople should not be the ones responsible for creating, developing, and maintaining sales tools—they are the users of these tools.

Complete the exercise in Figure 9.2 to raise your awareness about the ownership gaps for your consultative sales methodology and its related sales tools. Identify the entity in your organization that has (or should have) ownership for each item listed in the "sales tool" column. These departments or individuals should have assigned responsibility for designing, developing, and maintaining the sales tools, including the all-important sales process deliverables.

Whose Responsibility Is It Anyway?

Who should have responsibility for designing, developing, and maintaining sales tools? We surveyed several of our

FIGURE 9.2 Responsibility for Sales Tools

SALES TOOL	RESPONSIBLE DEPARTMENTS/ INDIVIDUALS

own clients, and their consensus was that responsibility should fall to the sales support staff in conjunction with the marketing department. Sales support can take on many meanings. Many of our clients have sales support departments responsible for demonstrations, presentations, and technical assistance, and, perhaps, a proposal department.

Consider how much time and effort it took to design and develop your company's Web site. Is a department or individual responsible for keeping the site's content current? How much does site design, development, and maintenance cost your company each year? Your corporate Web site is a marketing and sales tool. Just like a value estimation tool or sales intelligence system, it needs constant maintenance to be effective. Your Web site contains your corporate background information, news, and, perhaps, downloads. The content on the site must be kept current to stay effective.

Now, take a moment to think about these Web site development and maintenance questions you just answered and answer the following questions. Note the gaps that may exist between these answers and the answers to the questions listed above.

- How much time and effort did it take to design and develop the sales methodology and sales tools you use in your company's consultative sales process?
- Is a department or individual responsible for keeping your sales methodology and sales tools content current?

- How much does sales methodology and sales tool design, development, and maintenance cost your company each year?

The point is, companies spend thousands of dollars each year keeping their Web sites current with fresh information. They have a department or individual responsible for site design, development, and maintenance. Yet they allow their sales methodology and its related materials and tools to go stale.

Once again, create a list of your sales tools and deliverables that have no ownership responsibility and identify what departments or individuals should take ownership. Be sure to include the sales tools and sales process deliverables that aren't currently available—the ones you want and need to design and develop.

Take this ownership concept seriously. It represents a big gap for many selling organizations. It's one of the major reasons salespeople try to use generic sales tools and deliverables or attempt to create their own, causing the silo effect we discussed earlier. Do your sales professionals write their own proposals or develop their own ROI valuation tools? Does this make any sense to you? If your company spent as much on its sales methodology and sales tools as it does on its Web site, how much increased revenue might result?

Stuff You Need to Remember

The generic and missing sales tools are reflective of gaps in how some organizations have implemented their consultative sales methodologies. It seems that nobody in these organizations has taken the time to design the needed custom sales tools and process deliverables. Equally important, nobody has taken ownership for their design and maintenance. Consequently, sales professionals use sample materials from their sales training programs, rework product training and marketing materials, or struggle to create their own tools and deliverables.

✓ Engage your sales force and others within your company in analyzing your current situation.

✓ Compare the amount of money your company spends annually on its Web site to that spent maintaining its sales methodology and customized sales tools.

✓ Sales professionals should not be responsible for creating, developing, and maintaining sales tools, including sales process deliverables—they are users of these tools.

✓ Ownership is critical to a successful design, development, and deployment of custom sales tools.

10

Gluing It All Together

*"I caught him by surprise.
Nobody has ever tried to sell him three of anything."*

After being disappointed by Dave and Sara, Johnny de-cided to take his concerns and ideas to the top. The CIO replied to Johnny, "Your system will be perfect for our company, but any purchase of this magnitude requires a formal proposal and pre-sentation by me to the executive committee." Now Johnny needs more than his basic generic proposal template to close this deal.

From Johnny's perspective, he knows his proposal will have to convince the executive committee to approve the deal. Because he hasn't met with anyone on the committee, the proposal and presentation will have to educate them on the research Johnny performed regarding their company's current issues and the cost of doing nothing. Just as important, his proposal will need to show his product as the best value for their investment.

The bottom line for Johnny's deal, and many deals facing sales professionals like Johnny, is that prospective customers want and need sales proposals because their companies have internal spending and acquisition policies. Typically, any in-vestment over a certain dollar amount requires review and ap-proval by an executive committee or board of directors. The committee members need sufficient information to make in-formed business decisions. We believe a sales proposal is the best medium; a cover letter with a price quote and brochure in a folder is simply not enough to convince someone to spend sev-eral thousand dollars.

Johnny sent an e-mail to Dave and Sara requesting copies of past proposals he could emulate. Winning proposals were his preference. Johnny knows he will be competing against one other vendor. He hopes the other vendor will be scrambling as much as he is to write that winning proposal.

We include a separate chapter on sales proposals because of the critical role proposals play in many complex sales situations and consultative sales processes. Some companies let (or make) their sales professionals write their own proposals—which is inefficient, costly, and inconsistent with any corporate-branding initiative. This chapter will help you understand how and why your sales proposals might represent the most important sales process deliverables your company's sales professionals produce.

Purpose of a Sales Proposal—the Glue

If a sales professional follows a consultative sales methodology, then the sales proposal represents a logical deliverable for a prospective customer. Think about all the sales activities that a salesperson completes in the preceding phases, up to the point where the prospect is ready to make a decision. Prior to receiving a proposal, a prospect might have received the following documents and information from a salesperson:

- Business development letter
- Brochures
- Data sheets

- Confirmation letters
- ROI valuation
- Systems configuration
- Demonstration results
- Preliminary price or fee quote
- Case studies
- Customer and reference lists
- Preliminary implementation or installation plan

When the prospect is ready to make a decision, will he or she sort through the documents listed above trying to determine exactly how the seller's proposed solution will help resolve the problem? The seller's contact within the buying organization could provide the decision makers with copies of many of the output documents the seller provided. However, the issue for the seller is having no control over what the contact is providing. Therefore, writing a high-quality, custom proposal will ensure that the selling organization is represented in the very best manner. The proposal is the glue that pulls it all together: literature, configuration, declaration of key issues, value estimation, investment, and implementation, as well as the selling company's background.

Look at Johnny's situation: the CIO needs something to give her company's executive committee. He needs to package—actually, *repackage*—all the information he's gathered and processed and all his resulting recommendations so it paints a positive picture to the executives who will make the final decision. Therefore, Johnny's sales proposal has several primary purposes, it must

- document the results of preceding consultative sales activities;
- describe how Johnny's product features, and the resulting benefits, perfectly match the buyer's unique needs;
- define how the proposed product provides a compelling, buyer-specific financial justification; and
- assure the buyer that the seller is capable of delivering.

The Proposal Documents the Results— the Biggest Process Connections User

Selling consultatively is an essential ingredient for writing winning, buyer-focused sales proposals. As a sales professional works with the buyer, he or she will identify and define process connections information, which belong in a sales proposal. Figure 10.1 shows that a sales proposal represents the single biggest user of PCI.

A sales professional often works with one or two people from the buyer's organization—key contacts. Key contacts influence a buying decision, but they usually don't make it. Therefore, everything discussed and agreed to with the contact needs to be communicated to the decision makers for their review. A well-written sales proposal should contain

FIGURE 10.1 Sales Proposal and PCI

PROCESS CONNECTIONS INFORMATION

SALES TOOLS	Background Information	Critical Business Issues, KPIs	Impacts on Business	Customer's Needs	Customer's Selection Criteria	Product/Service Application	Prices/Fees	Nonfinancial Benefits	Financial Benefits	Implementation/ Installation Variables
Sales Proposal	U	U	U	U	U	U	U	U	U	U

everything, all the PCI a decision maker needs to make an informed business decision.

The Proposal Matches Needs to Benefits

Selling consultatively includes defining a buyer's needs. Some consultative sales methodologies consider a buyer's needs to represent its ideas for a solution. Therefore, if you can clearly define a buyer's needs, what the buyer thinks represents a solution, you can match these needs to the benefits provided by your product features or service capabilities. In other words, by clearly defining the buyer's needs in your proposal, you can "set the stage" for your proposed product or service and its value proposition. If this is done correctly, you can position your product or service as a perfect fit for the prospective customer. A consultative selling approach, followed by the effective use of PCI in a proposal, results in a compelling process deliverable—a buyer-focused sales proposal.

The Proposal Defines Financial Justification

Certainly one of the most important purposes of a proposal is to describe how your proposed product or service reduces expenses, avoids costs, or increases revenues—more PCI. A sales proposal should specifically identify and explain the money-saving or moneymaking benefits the buyer will realize. Your custom ROI valuation uses the prospect's key pain indicators as a basis for these calculations. This buyer-specific ROI information belongs in a sales proposal. Obviously, you can't convince a decision maker with industry averages, vague examples, or constructed case studies.

It Also Reduces the Risk

Most buyers face risk when making a change. For example, implementing a new system, installing a new machine, or hiring a new (and unknown) CPA firm represent decisions that carry risk. Business risk becomes a factor in the decision process because most companies aren't eager to jeopardize their success. Your contacts and the decision makers also have personal risk for recommending or making a wrong decision. Therefore, to reduce the buyer's risk, a proposal should present some information about the seller and its capabilities—it should assure the buyer that the seller is experienced and knows what it's doing.

A sales proposal itself can assure a buyer of the seller's capabilities. A proposal's general appearance and its overall quality will send subtle messages to the buyer. Its flow of information and ideas, writing style, format, paper quality, and binding tell the buyer a lot about the selling organization.

Danger, Everyone Is Writing Proposals

When the company lets its sales professionals write their own sales proposals, it potentially can create some serious problems and some poor-quality documents. In most situations, the sales proposal is a sales process deliverable and often also represents the first deliverable from the seller to the buyer's decision makers. Does a poor-quality proposal mean that the company's products or services will also have quality issues? Not necessarily. But a poor-quality proposal may raise these types of questions with the buyer's decision makers. Why would a company take that risk? Remember: *a proposal doesn't have to be good, just PERFECT!*

Here are some of the possible dangers if sales profession-als write their own proposals:

- Not all sales professionals are good writers, which means their sales proposals will not read very well.
- Their proposals might not have a professional look and feel. If salespeople have trouble formatting large documents, especially when they are in the "cut and paste" mode, the resulting documents will reflect badly on the company.
- If sales professionals cut and paste more than they write, some of the content will not exactly match their buyer's unique situations. The concept that "it is close enough, the buyers will get the general idea" doesn't make it.
- Sales professionals may forget to include the latest system options, or more important, they may forget to include the disclaimer statement that the legal department wanted in all sales proposals.

Who's Selling Boilerplate?

We mentioned in an earlier chapter that a proposal where most of the wording is the same for all buyers is a boilerplate proposal. Typically, the only difference from one boilerplate proposal and the next is the buyer's name and the price. To write a boilerplate proposal, a salesperson only needs to

download the latest version of the company's boilerplate proposal document, make a few changes, and the proposal's
done. Boilerplate proposals are easy to write and can look
good—there is no cutting and pasting or formatting. However, boilerplate proposals send the wrong messages to buyers:

- *All buyers are alike.* Buyers have unique business operations, different critical business issues, and unique
  business needs and objectives. If a salesperson uses a
  boilerplate proposal, especially after following a consultative sales methodology, it represents a major disconnect for the buyer. The buyer will wonder what
  happened to all the information gathered, discussed,
  and agreed upon during the many meetings.
- *Just another peddler.* A sales professional who uses a
  boilerplate proposal has little credibility with the
  buyer and becomes just another peddler.
- *Peddling a commodity.* A boilerplate proposal will
  quickly commoditize most products or services. It
  may force the buyer to differentiate more on price
  and availability because the seller doesn't think the
  buyer's operations, critical issues, and the application
  of its proposed product or service really matters. At
  least, the seller's boilerplate proposal reads that way,
  and that's what the decision makers are reading.

Many companies use boilerplate proposals, even ones
that sell very complex products or services. These companies

probably have some logical reasons for using boilerplate proposals—at least someone in the company thinks it's logical. Perhaps they want to make sure their sales professionals

- deliver the same "factory-approved" sales message every time, even though all prospective buyers are different;
- include standardized wording because it must satisfy a legal or regulatory issue—so let's standardize the whole thing; or
- don't spend too much time writing sales proposals and don't have to sell consultatively—just tell the salespeople to give the sales support assistant the buyer's name and the price, and the assistant will get you the proposal tomorrow morning.

Put yourself on the buyer's side of the desk after getting a boilerplate proposal. You might think a nice brochure and a price quote would serve the same purpose—perhaps better.

Tip: See the Buyer . . . Be the Buyer

The most important tip we can give you for writing a winning sales proposal is to write from the buyer's viewpoint. Pretend you're the buyer, it's your money, and you have to make the decision. What would you want to know? Here are some other tips to help you write a proposal from the buyer's viewpoint:

- *Provide a logical flow of information and ideas.* From a reader's perspective, a sales proposal should have a logical flow of information and ideas. It should glue everything together and be easy to follow and understand. Design your proposal so it groups similar types of PCI. For example, buyer information, proposed solution, implementation, seller profile, and business considerations create a nice flow.

- *Educate the decision makers.* Pretend you're one of the buyer's decision makers who has little or no knowledge about the specific business function or operation discussed. Use the proposal to educate the decision makers—they'll appreciate it. Never assume the decision makers have the same knowledge level about every aspect of their business or some particular business issue facing their company.

- *Don't make it too long.* Don't write a proposal that is so long it becomes a major project to read it. You want the decision makers to read the proposal (or at least skim through and hit the important stuff). Of course, the complexity of your proposed product or service and the business issues facing the buyer will affect length. Avoid lengthy product descriptions, specifications, or implementation task lists in the main body. Instead, summarize this material and put the details in appendixes.

One of our clients, Bombardier Flexjet, sells fractional ownership of business jets to corporations and affluent individuals. Shortly after starting with Flexjet, Bob Knebel, VP of sales, recognized the need to introduce a consultative sales methodology and develop proposal models to align with the methodology. Flexjet now uses one of the leading consultative sales methodologies. Its new sales directors receive individualized training in the methodology, and everyone receives periodic refresher training from a consultant who is very familiar with its business. The sales directors use the methodology's generic client questionnaire.

Bob realized their proposals were abbreviated; they contained little more than a price, fees, and some prospect-specific information. He wanted the proposals to communicate the *Flexjet experience* and reflect the high service levels Flexjet provides its owners. We designed, developed, and automated several proposal models. We also designed a supplement to the generic questionnaire to help Flexjet sales directors define buyer information specific to the sale of business jets. Flexjet used marketing and other resources to design a very impressive binder and package.

(Continued)

Flexjet's sales training consultant attended our rollout session and commented afterward, "I train the sales directors how to collect, understand, and process the prospect information in the questionnaire, now they have a place to use it." The new proposals do exactly what Bob intended them to do; they reinforce Flexjet's sales methodology and reflect the *Flexjet experience*. The bottom line is they produce better results. Several sales directors have proposal close ratios of 80 percent or higher.

How Effective Is Your Company's Proposal Production Process?

Take the survey in Figure 10.2 to see if your sales proposals need some help.

Then look at survey responses and some diagnostic and prescriptive information.

FIGURE 10.2 Proposal Survey

1. Do you cut and paste sections from past sales proposals when you write a new one?	___ Yes ___ No
2. Can you write a new sales proposal by just changing the buyer's name and the price—boilerplate proposals?	___ Yes ___ No
3. How long does it typically take and how much does it cost to generate a proposal?	___ Less than 1 hour ___ 1–2 hours ___ 2–3 hours ___ 3–4 hours ___ 4–5 hours ___ 6 or more hours _____ Cost
4. How many people in your organization write proactive proposals?	_____

1. Do You Cut and Paste Sections from Past Sales Proposals When You Write a New One?

- *Yes.* Your proposals might not: a) provide the reader with a logical flow of information, b) contain very much customer-specific information, or c) completely reflect the message your company wants to communicate to its prospective customers.
- *No.* Your sales professionals probably write proposals by using a company model that follows an approved structure and contains approved content.

2. Can You Write a New Sales Proposal by Just Changing the Buyer's Name and the Price?

- *Yes.* You probably are writing boilerplate proposals, which send a message that all buyers are alike. Remember, if you are following a consultative sales process, your boilerplate proposals reflect a major disconnect for your buyers.

- *No.* You are definitely not writing boilerplate proposals. If you are following a consultative sales process, your proposals probably contain customer-specific information.

3. How Long Does It Take and How Much Does It Cost to Generate a Proposal?

If your sales professionals write proposals, it can be very costly for your company. For example, if a sales professional has a base salary of $60,000 and benefits add another 25 percent, his or her fully loaded annual cost is $60,000 × 1.25 = $75,000 (before commissions). There are approximately 1,950 working hours in a year, so the fully loaded hourly rate for this sales professional is approximately $38.50. If it takes three hours to write a proposal, it costs $115.50 before printing, packaging, and shipping. What's the *average, fully loaded base salary* and *hourly cost* for one of your sales professionals?

$_____$ / year divided by 1,950 hours /
year equals a cost of $_____$ / hour.

It's difficult to measure the opportunity cost when the sales professional is writing a proposal; he or she is not selling. However, one might look at a sales professional's opportunity costs as the amount of revenue he or she generates each year divided by 1,950 hours. Therefore, a sales professional with a $750,000 quota would have an hourly opportunity cost of approximately $385.00 per hour. Writing proposals is a very expensive process from this viewpoint.

What's the *average quota* and *hourly opportunity cost* for one of your sales professionals?

$_____$ / year divided by 1,950 hours /
year equals a cost of $_____$ / hour.

Calculate your per-proposal costs (see Figure 10.3).

4. How Many People in Your Organization Write Proactive Proposals?

Does automating proposal production make sense for your company? We just talked with a company that has about 50 sales professionals who write more than 7,500 proposals each year. A conservative total cost estimate for writing proposals approaches $600,000 annually. They didn't

FIGURE 10.3 Proposal Costs

TIME TO WRITE ONE PROPOSAL	COST @ $80,000/ YEAR (Fully Loaded Base)	COST @ $750,000 (Annual Quota)	YOUR COSTS @ $_____ / YEAR (Fully Loaded Base)	YOUR COSTS @ $_____ / YEAR (Average Annual Quota)
1 hour	$40.00	$385.00	_____	_____
2 hours	$80.00	$770.00	_____	_____
3 hours	$120.00	$1,155.00	_____	_____
4 hours	$160.00	$1,540.00	_____	_____
6 hours	$240.00	$2,370.00	_____	_____
8 hours	$320.00	$3,080.00	_____	_____

want to know the opportunity cost; however, we did, and it was over $6 million!

If more than five salespeople in your company write sales proposals, it can be cost-effective to automate the process, especially if they each write more than two proposals a month. An automated system can significantly reduce proposal production times. For example, if it takes a sales professional four hours to write a proposal using a word processing system (probably cutting and pasting), and by using an automated proposal production system, the production time can be reduced to one hour, then the three-hour savings mean a cost savings of $120 (fully loaded cost) to $1,155 (opportunity cost) per proposal. If the company has eight sales professionals who each writes only one proposal per month, then the company could save $960 to $9,240 per month with an automated system—lots of reduced costs to acquire a system or service. Besides saving time and money, automating the proposal production process ensures consistency of content—all sales proposals contain the same company-approved message.

Stuff You Need to Remember

If a salesperson follows a consultative sales methodology, then the sales proposal represents a logical deliverable for a prospective customer. It's reasonable for a prospect to want something that glues all the pieces together after the sales professional has completed his or her sales activities.

- ✓ A winning sales proposal connects the sales professional and selling organization with the buyer's decision makers and provides them with all the information they need to make an informed buying decision.
- ✓ A sales proposal is the single biggest user of process connections information.
- ✓ In most situations, the sales proposal represents the first deliverable from the seller to the buyer's decision makers—it doesn't have to be good, just perfect.
- ✓ A sales proposal must educate the buyer's decision makers and provide them with a logical flow of

information and ideas on which to make an informed decision.

✓ When the company lets its salespeople write their own sales proposals, it should expect that not all of its proposals will meet quality standards for content and appearance—it should expect to see some pretty bad proposals.

✓ Boilerplate proposals are easy to write and probably look good; however, they send the wrong messages to buyers.

✓ Automating the proposal production process will reduce production times and costs while ensuring consistency and quality.

11

What to Do About It

"Sir, the buyer will see you now."

Johnny knew he still needed to get Dave and Sara on board, and with his "gap" list of what he felt was missing in his sales tool arsenal, Johnny now had a clear outline of what he needed to succeed. Reflecting on what he'd done to date, he realized he had taken it as far as he could on his own. First, he had developed several sales tools and semicustomized the sales methodology that was forced upon him. He had continued to build additional sales tools by drawing from his own experience and referencing some classic best-selling books. But to build an entirely customized and integrated sales methodology complete with tools, Johnny needed larger support from the corporation, and he needed Dave and Sara to commit to it. He had the gap list and a plan of action. The question remained, was Johnny going to get the money and marketing support he needed?

The Quick Fix Doesn't Exist

There is no quick fix for an organization whose sales methodology, process, and sales tools are not customized and integrated. In this chapter, we turn to many experts and past exercises to help you assess your current situation.

At ROI4Sales, part of our marketing campaign is to send outbound e-mails to a focus list in our prospect database on a regular basis. This continuous e-mail campaign keeps our database current and helps us build awareness in our target market. The sales force carries on this campaign, which has little or no cost to the organization. We do, however, provide give-away items (e.g., white papers, research papers, articles, and, of course, one of our books) for the sales force to use to get a better response. Recently, one of our sales professionals sent the following e-mail. Pay special attention to the response he received from a sales rep in the field.

Subject: How effective are your ROI sales tools?

Joe,

How do you know your value estimation or ROI sales tools are effective?

We have researched many value estimation or sales tools from individuals, small companies, research firms, and large Fortune 50 companies, and many in between, and believe the effectiveness of ROI or value estimation in (and after) the sales process boils down to these nine very important criteria:

- Objectivity
- Credibility
- Graphics
- Accuracy
- Educational effectiveness
- Creative output
- Cost and benefit represented
- Ability to use ROI throughout and after the sale
- Documentation and training

Let me know if you would like the "How effective are your ROI sales tools?" research paper. It will help you grade the quality & effectiveness of your current tools.

Thanks,
John

The following e-mail response came back to John.

Subject: How effective are your ROI sales tools?

John,

You didn't hear this from me; but I have no such tools. Try sending this to Fred@abccompany.com and see if you get something. I do the best I can with the "tools" I'm provided and frankly have found that my complaining about the tools or lack of hasn't served my standing in the company. I'm just a "sales guy" and don't have control of such decisions.

Good luck and please, again, keep this confidential as to how you got his e-mail address.

Joe

As you can see from his response, Joe is frustrated. Ask yourself, is this you? Is this your sales force? What can you do if you are "just" a sales guy? We believe the only thing worse than investing in your sales force and risking them leaving the organization is to not invest and have them stay. That's right, a frustrated salesperson like Joe is likely causing all sorts of issues within your own company. With an average tenure of two to three years for enterprise sales professionals, you undoubtedly have a significant investment in their success. Remember the statistic that 25 percent of salespeople fail from poor attitude. Well, frustration is a major cause of that.

What Do I Need to Do First?

Analyzing the Numbers

In Chapters 3, 6, and 8, we asked that you perform a self-assessment of your current situation. Refer back to those scores and enter them into Figure 11.2 along with your score from the assessment in Figure 11.1. This exercise helps you to assess your current situation as it relates to your organization's commitment to the success of your sales force. The individual totals for each of the four categories are described in the chapters themselves and can provide a picture of how healthy you are in that particular area of interest. However, the cumulative points indicate your opportunity for success based on historical research.

The total number of points is less important than the individual scores as they relate to each other. It is important to understand specifically where you are deficient. For example, if you scored 24 points by scoring a 8 in Methodology, 8 in Sales Tools, 7 in Training, and 1 in Integration, then

FIGURE 11.1 Sales Training Assessment Chart

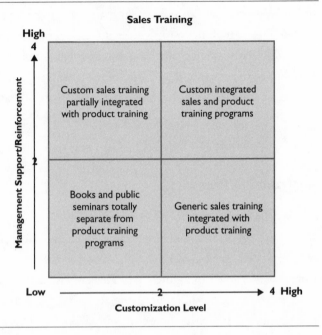

Sales Training

Books and public seminars totally separate from product training programs

Custom sales training partially integrated with product training

Custom integrated sales and product training programs

Generic sales training integrated with product training

FIGURE 11.2 Total Score

Enter the number of points scored for Sales Methodology: _____

Enter the number of points scored for Sales Tools: _____

Enter the number of points scored for Integration: _____

Enter the number of points scored for Sales Training: _____

Total points scored: _____

clearly you have an issue with Integration and need to deal specifically with that. However, if you scored a 16, with 4 in each category, your issues are spread across all of the categories and will require a more global approach to correct them. The ideal score is 28 or greater across all four categories. This being said, we suggest you first identify the areas of deficiency you need to correct. If you are deficient in more than one area, prioritize your efforts in this order: Sales Methodology, Tools, Integration, and Training.

Sales Methodology

There is no shortage of high-quality sales methodologies. Mahan Khalsa, in *Let's Get Real or Let's Not Play*, wrote, "With due respect to true sales professionals, the notion of sales and selling carries a lot of negative baggage. It is the second oldest profession, often confused with the first. No matter what you put in front or in back of the word selling (consultative, solution, visionary, creative, integrity, value-based, beyond), it still ends up with the sense of doing something 'to' somebody rather than 'for' or 'with' somebody."

While this may be true, a change in thought is necessary to achieve true partnership. To shift your prospects' fear of being "sold to," you will want to develop a relationship that withstands the test of time. This includes a consultative approach to your sales effort. Refer to our Resources section for a list of several consultative sales methodologies and recommendations based on the size of your sales staff, your budget, and the complexity of your products or services. If you are interviewing companies, remember to include the following questions in your evaluation process:

- How much research do you perform on a company prior to training its sales force?
- Do you offer "executive" training?
- Do you offer training for "nonsales" personnel?
- Do you customize your training to our products and services?
- Do you customize your sales tools to fit each company and its products and services?
- Do you include the use of these customized sales tools and other resources in a typical training course?
- Does your training course include lead-generation techniques?

These questions don't include all of the information you will need to objectively evaluate a sales methodology, but they are a good start. Ask all the references about customization and their results since the training session. According to research by CSO Insights, "More than 85 percent of companies that provide custom sales methodology training to their sales staff experience an improvement in revenue."

Sales Tools

The second most important item on your priority list is the development, integration, and deployment of custom sales tools into your sales methodology. Regardless of the product or service you sell, you will need custom tools to be successful.

When evaluating sales tools, keep the following points in mind:

- Assign ownership to someone or a department—this person or group must keep each sales tool accurate and current.
- Always ask about training—most sales tools are not used or are misused because of a lack of training.
- Be sure you can customize each sales tool to your environment—ensure you or the vendor is capable of customizing each tool without significant cost or training lead times.
- Ensure management has bought in to the decision to purchase or develop the sales tools—lack of management commitment will assuredly cause the demise of even the best tools.
- It is essential that your sales tools are of the highest quality—they must be accurate, easy to use, deliver value to the recipient, and assist in moving a sale forward.

We encourage you to focus on accuracy, objectivity, and credibility. If your sales tools include these attributes, you are headed in the right direction. See the Resources section in the back of this book for more ideas on tools and tool development.

Integration

There are two elements to integration: physical and methodical. This book is primarily about methodically integrating your custom sales methodology, process, and tools. However, we don't want to minimize the need for assistance from inside or outside your organization to physically integrate all your sales tools into your methodology and process.

As discussed in previous chapters, there is a need to create process connections information in one tool, a source, and use that information in another tool—this integration provides an efficiency improvement in the overall sales process.

> Only about 54 percent of those polled capture vital customer information, including PCI, in a CRM system.

Team selling is a revitalized concept. We see a significant increase in the use of team selling techniques in the complex sale. Each member of the sales team has a role, a responsibility, and a prospect intelligence assignment. There is a desire and need to be able to share PCI among the team members and the prospect. Without a method to share data, analyze results, and provide high-quality process deliverables, it would be impossible to succeed in a complex sale. Physical integration and a central repository for the information are crucial.

It is more common than you think to see companies collect data in one system and reenter it multiple times in other systems. Physical integration will affect several factors throughout the sales process, such as accuracy of data as it moves through the sales process, awareness throughout the organization, productivity improvements, implementation and postsale quality improvements, and litigation cost reductions.

Most organizations we talk to use or are preparing to use a CRM and/or an SFA system. The sophistication of these systems allows them to be the repository for much of the data collected throughout the sales process. These systems offer the perfect opportunity to become the hub for much of the PCI and to integrate sales tools with a sales methodology. When reviewing SFA systems, aside from the ability to customize, we suggest you look for these features to make your life easier:

- Automatically send literature
- Create and send sales process letters
- Create survey screens to collect survey data
- Automatically export data to a value estimation model, configuration system, and sales proposal and other document production systems
- Create custom e-mail campaigns
- Track competition
- Define stages and steps in sales process
- Automate "triggers" based on stages achieved

An SFA system is only one way to integrate all of your tools. There are many other options available to you. Smaller organizations may choose to use Microsoft CRM, Business Contact Manager, or even Microsoft Excel or ACT, for example. The most important factor is that you make the effort to minimize duplicate data entry and collect the information necessary to assess, prescribe, and deploy your solution to your prospects.

Training

The only reason that training is the fourth priority is that without the other three priorities, there would be no need for training. Don't minimize its importance. According to the American Society of Training and Development (ASTD), only 39 percent of U.S. companies provide sales training to their selling organizations. In *Strategies to Win Sales,* Mark Marone and Seleste Lunsford point out, "Even then, training often is focused on product knowledge—even at the expense of selling skills and sales processes." This is a problem for both the organization and the individual.

The need for training is essential to the success of a consultative selling approach. As of this writing, there are ten colleges in the United States that offer a degree in sales. This is a problem when two out of every three college graduates become salespeople or become involved in their company's sales processes.

Without training, misusing sales tools is as bad as not using the sales tool at all. Due to a lack of training or understanding, for example, many sales professionals will use the wrong tool, therefore overlooking critical information needed to complete the sales process.

There are many methods for training available: computer-based, instructor-led, Internet-based, or via Internet radio (e.g., *www.salesrepradio.com*). Be sure to research all of your options. We are huge supporters of the Web-based seminar or Webcast. Usually they are free and only take an hour. For instance, Net Briefings (*www.netbriefings.com*), Progressive Business (*www.pbconferences.com*), Sales Performance International (*www.spisales.com*), and Microsoft all offer Web-based seminars.

When interviewing a training organization, remember to ask the following questions:

- What is the best size for a class to be the most productive?
- Do you incorporate our custom sales tools in your sales training?
- Do you provide customized training programs focused on our products and services?
- Do you provide executive daily debriefs after each day of training?
- Do you provide a copy of all training materials up front?
- What is the recommended instructor-to-student ratio?
- Do you incorporate videotaping in your training? (This is one of the most effective training tools available.)
- Is your training staff required to complete a certification program that incorporates a minimum number of hours spent working with the subject matter?

Many training programs target a subject and omit the surrounding material. Custom sales training must incorporate the custom sales tools used throughout your sales process. If your sales training vendor does not understand this point, look for a new one.

How Big of a Job Is It?

Use Figure 11.3 to assess where you are currently and how large of a change is ahead of you and your company.

If you had a perfect score, which would be two, then you have nothing to do—everything is in place and customized perfectly for your organization. Just make sure you have the

---

FIGURE 11.3 Questionnaire to Determine Company Status

On a scale of 1 to 10, where 1 is very little and 10 is very much, how much do you need to customize the consultative sales methodology used by your company to sell its products and services?   _____

On a scale of 1 to 10, where 1 is very customized and 10 is not at all customized, how customized is the consultative sales training program that your company provides its sales professionals?   _____

How many sales tools do you need to develop? (Refer to Chapter 9.)   _____

How many existing sales tools do you need to customize?   _____

How many other sales tools or systems (e.g., system configuration, ROI valuation, sales proposal production) does your company need to design and develop or acquire?   _____

How many sales tools have no department or individual responsible for their initial design and development and ongoing maintenance?   _____

Total: _____

---

resources in place to maintain everything. However, if your score is more than 20, you have some significant work ahead. If your score is 40 or more, you should expect to assign a dedicated staff to a major project and you may want to use outside resources.

Defining Project Scope

To accurately define the project scope, you'll need to return to a chart first introduced in Figure 8.3. Here, we've added a Sales Component Variable category with three columns to help identify each sales tool's type (tool or deliverable), its current availability, and whether it needs to be customized. The Availability and Customized columns will help define project scope.

The sample Sales Phase-Tools-Process Connections table (Figure 11.4) uses our generic sales process phases and some typical sales tools and process connections. Within the Sales Component Variable category, it's important to note that visually checking the Availability column makes it easy to identify the sales tools that need to be designed and developed or acquired. A sales tool with a blank Availability cell means it will need to be included in the project. In our example table, we have nine blank cells and, therefore, we have nine sales tools that we need to design and develop or acquire. Also, all components with an "R" in the Customized column must be included

FIGURE 11.4 Sample Sales Phase-Tools-Process Connections Table

SALES TOOL	COMPONENT VARIABLES			PROCESS CONNECTIONS											SALES PROCESS PHASE							
	Tool or Deliverable (T or D)	Available (Y = Yes; blank = No)	Customized (N = Now; R = Required)	Background Information	Critical Business Issues	Impacts on Business	Key Pains	Customer Needs	Customer's Selection Criteria	Product Application	Prices/Fees	Nonfinancial Benefits	Financial Benefits	Implementation Variables	Target	Qualify	Meet/Greet	Presentation	Proposal	Due Diligence	Close	Postsales
Customer Intelligence	T	Y	N/A	S			S								X	X						
Prospect Questionnaire	T	Y	R	S	S	S	S	S	S			S				X	X	X				
ROI Questionnaire	T		R			S	S			U	U		B			X	X	X				
Sales Proposal	D	Y	R	U	U	U	U	U	U	U	U	U	U	U					X	X	X	
CRM/SFA	T	Y	N	R	R	R	R	R	R	R	R	R	R	R	X	X	X	X	X	X	X	X

S = Source; U = Use; B = Both; R = Repository

in the project because they are either currently available only as *generic* components or not available.

Fill in a Sales Phase-Tools-Process Connections table for your company. If you have been doing the exercises in the preceding chapters, you should be able to complete this table in record time. Even though you filled in most of the information used in this table in previous chapters, completing this "final" table for your company is a good review exercise. You might want to have several people within your organization help you complete the table, or you might ask them to complete a table independently and compare the results.

Important Considerations before Defining the Project

You're almost ready to define the activities and resource requirements for your project. However, the table you just completed doesn't reveal the current customization level of your consultative sales methodology and corresponding sales training programs. The table does show the following important interdependencies: 1) which custom sales tools your company needs to support its sales process, 2) in what phase or phases these sales tools are used, and 3) which sales tools are sources or uses of PCI.

Defining your company's sales tools and their characteristics begins to move your company to a more custom application of its consultative sales methodology. There's no doubt that designing and developing (or acquiring) custom sales tools represents a major step towards the custom application of your consultative sales methodology.

To sell consultatively, sales professionals must be able to use their company's custom sales tools. Will your project need to include the development of custom training programs? You better plan on it and budget for it, too. Making new sales tools available doesn't mean your sales professionals will know how to use them. Your project must incorporate the design and development of initial and ongoing training programs.

However, there is some good news. Since you'll be training your sales professionals to use your company's custom sales tools, by default, your training also will be custom.

Outsource, Outhouse, or In-House?

Here's where you start to test management's commitment level. If you're facing a major project, you'll need resources from other departments and a budget, especially if you're going to use outside resources. You'll have to sell the project internally and you'll need a project plan.

A project plan (see Figure 11.5) should include phases, activities by phase, resource requirements, deliverables, and a schedule.

Next, let's add some more detail to our project plan (see Figure 11.6):

- *Deliverables* means the outputs or outcomes of each phase.
- *Assigned* identifies the persons or functional areas needed to complete the phase activities.
- *Estimated duration* represents the estimated length of each phase. Note: Our duration estimates are just that. The actual duration of a phase is dependent upon available resources, resource commitment levels, and amount of work needed to be completed.

Your preliminary plan should include all the specifics as they relate to your company. Further, the project plan and budget you and the project team develop must identify and include your company's unique sales tools development or acquisition requirements.

In the Resources section in the back of this book, we provide a list of resources you can use to build up your customized sales tools, sales methodology, and sales training program. Also, visit *www.whyjohnnycantsell.com* to purchase the *Why Johnny Can't Sell* Project Team Pack.

FIGURE 11.5 Project Plan

PHASE	ACTIVITIES	COMMENTS/RECOMMENDATIONS
Project Planning	• Assemble project team • Develop project plan • Refine internal and external project resource requirements • Refine project budget	• Make sure your team includes representatives from all of the departments that will contribute to content. • Make sure you synchronize the project plan and budget.
Functional Design	• Define sales methodology requirements and processes • Decide if the current sales methodology will work, needs customization, or needs to be scraped and new one acquired • Define custom sales tools and their initial development and ongoing maintenance responsibilities • Define process connections information for each sales tool and within the process • Decide which sales tools will be designed and developed internally and which will be acquired • Identify which existing sales tools and processes need to be customized	• Use or revise the table you completed in the exercise from this chapter as your starting point. • Make sure all team members understand sale tools and PCI.
Design and Development	• Acquire/design/develop/customize sales methodologies, process, and tools	• Make sure the sales methodology and its processes are customized before working on the sales tools. • Developing some individual sales tools might represent a project within the project, especially if you are developing a major component. • The project manager will need to coordinate outside resources, if used, with internal subject matter experts.

FIGURE 11.5 Project Plan *(Continued)*

PHASE	ACTIVITIES	COMMENTS/RECOMMENDATIONS
Testing	• Test sales process and tools • Revise sales processes and tools as needed	• Unit-test each process and sales tool with live prospects and assigned sales professionals—make sure everything works in the real world.
Develop Training Programs	• Develop/revise sales methodology training program • Develop training programs for sales tools	• Training resources should be involved in the entire project starting with the first phase; don't bring them into the project just for this phase. • The goal should be to integrate sales and product or service training; remember training on most custom sales tools will contribute to that goal.
Implementation	• Introduce your custom sales methodology • Introduce the custom sales tools • Deliver the custom training programs	• Use marketing to help promote the project and the training programs. • Make sure the sales professionals understand the scope and magnitude of the project and its intended benefits.
Operation	• Continually monitor and reinforce the use of consultative sales methodology • Maintain sales tools and training programs • Provide ongoing training	• The project creates a new sales environment for the company; the end of the project is not an event, it's the beginning of an ongoing process. • Make sure everyone understands the importance of ownership responsibilities for the sales tools.

FIGURE 11.6 More Detailed Project Plan

PHASE	ACTIVITIES	DELIVERABLES	ASSIGNED
Project Planning (Estimated Duration: 1–2 weeks)	• Assemble project team • Develop project plan • Refine internal and external project resource requirements • Develop a preliminary list of sales tools needed • Develop a project budget	• Project plan • Project budget	• Team • Project manager
Functional Design (2–6 weeks)	• Define sales methodology requirements and processes • Decide if the current sales methodology will work, needs customization, or needs to be scraped and new one acquired • Define custom sales tools and their initial development and ongoing maintenance responsibilities • Define process connections information for each sales tool and within the process • Decide which sales tools will be designed and developed internally and which will be acquired • Identify which existing sales tools and processes need to be customized	• Sales Phase-Tool-Process matrix • Acquisition list for sales tools	• Team • Project manager

FIGURE 11.6 More Detailed Project Plan (*Continued*)

PHASE	ACTIVITIES	DELIVERABLES	ASSIGNED
Design and Development (6–12 weeks)	• Acquire/design/develop/customize sales methodologies, process, and tools	• Internally developed sales tools • Acquired sales tools	• Sales • Marketing • Professional services • Product development
Testing (4–8 weeks)	• Test sales process and tools • Revise sales processes and tools as needed	• Tested sales tools	• Project manager • Internal subject matter experts • Outside resources
Develop Training Programs (4–6 weeks)	• Develop/revise sales methodology training program • Develop training programs for sales tools	• Custom sales methodology training program and materials • Custom sales tool training programs	• Same as design and development phase, plus sales professionals
Implementation (4–8 weeks)	• Introduce your custom sales methodology • Introduce the custom sales tools • Deliver the custom training programs	• Sales professionals trained on new custom methodology and sales tools for company's products and services	• Training • Sales • Professional services • Product development • Outside resources

FIGURE 11.6 More Detailed Project Plan *(Continued)*

PHASE	ACTIVITIES	DELIVERABLES	ASSIGNED
Ongoing Operation (Ongoing)	• Continually monitor and reinforce the use of consultative sales methodology • Maintain sales tools and training programs • Provide ongoing training • Define sales methodology requirements and processes • Decide if the current sales methodology will work, needs customization, or needs to be scraped and new one acquired • Define custom sales tools and their initial development and ongoing maintenance responsibilities • Define process connections information for each sales tool and within the process • Decide which sales tools will be designed and developed internally and which will be acquired • Identify which existing sales tools and processes need to be customized	• Consultative sales process activities • Maintained sales tools • Training for new hires • Updated sales tool training as needed	• Sales management • Sales support • Marketing • Training • Professional services • Product development or management • Outside resources

Stuff You Need to Remember

For those selling organizations that have been merely talking the talk, it's going to be a big and expensive project to fix their gaps. Other companies might simply need to design, develop, or customize a few sales tools.

✓ Make sure you thoroughly and accurately complete a Sales Phase-Tools-Process Connections table to define the scope and magnitude of the project.

✓ The development and use of custom sales tools will by default lead to a more custom application of any consultative sales mythology.

✓ Because your custom sales tools have been designed specifically to sell your company's products or services, then you must develop custom training programs to show your sales professionals how to use your sales tools; by definition, your sales professionals will receive integrated sales and product training.

✓ If you're facing a major project, don't try to do it on your own. You'll need management commitment, resources from other departments, and a budget if you're going to use outside resources. You might also have to sell the project internally.

Afterword

So Where Is Johnny Now?

We leave Johnny at a crossroads. Will he succeed? Will he get the desperately needed support from management and marketing? Does he have a shot?

There are two paths all Johnnys seem to take.

The first: his career could take off. (Hey, it's possible!)

Johnny might research the market to create a targeted list of a couple of hundred prospects that "could buy" from his new firm. Then he would probably develop a questionnaire to survey both customers and prospects on why they would buy this new product. Although this exercise would be a little time-consuming, it would help him understand the issues, pains, and goals his target market faces and how to position his new products when he calls on his focus list.

On this path to success, Johnny must work with Sara to create a marketing plan that would incorporate much of the research Johnny did. Their marketing program would focus on getting the target list to talk with Johnny about their critical business issues. As the leads would begin to flow in, Johnny would likely contact each firm and arrange for a time to meet and discuss their unique situation. The tools Johnny developed to capture critical business issues and cost of status quo would prove invaluable during the presentation phase of the sales process. Finally, Johnny most certainly would recruit Dave to help close the biggest sale in company history. Johnny and Dave now would be heroes.

Dave surely would like the fact that Johnny did his research and worked with marketing (Sara) to develop a plan of action. Dave would also like being engaged in each sale. Dave would realize Johnny's sales tools were effective ways of managing and controlling the sales process. He would agree to invest in more customization and more people. (Who wouldn't, with such great results?!) Johnny is probably now managing a large growing sales force.

Or, conversely, there's scenario two.

Perhaps Johnny haphazardly researches the market to create a target list of a couple of thousand prospects that "could buy" from his new firm. He probably would then ask Sara to develop a questionnaire they could use to survey customers and prospects. This exercise would be expensive and time-consuming and likely wouldn't prove to be of any value to Sara or Johnny.

Johnny didn't really connect with Sara and likely wouldn't work with her to develop any sort of marketing plan—like Johnny of old, he would probably try to do it himself. Johnny would probably try some half-baked plan to outsource calls to firms on his focus list to arrange for a time to meet. (We know how he hates to cold call.) Johnny probably wouldn't get any input from Dave or Sara or their customers and they would end up being inadequate. Finally, Johnny would spend a lot of time on the golf course working on his handicap.

Without larger internal support (in the form of budget for resources and staff) from management, Johnny would pretty much unravel. Dave and Johnny would likely refer to their lack of connection or success as "creative differences" and Johnny would be ready to quit and look for a new job. The outstanding question would be: Which would come first—would he quit or be fired?

So then, is Johnny a success story or cautionary tale? Well, both. Are you a Johnny, or do you employ one (or several)? It is not impossible to have a successful sales team, with the right tools and commitment. But no Johnny can go it alone.

Glossary

blog a personal or noncommercial Web site that uses a dated log format and contains links to other Web sites, along with commentary about those sites; blogs are updated frequently and sometimes group links by specific subjects, such as politics, news, pop culture, or computer issues; often used as an online diary of thoughts, ideas, and opinions.

boilerplate proposal a proposal in which most of the wording is the same for all buyers; typically, the only difference from one boilerplate proposal to the next is the buyer's name and the price.

business issue the quantifiable, logical explanation for the problem, issue, or goal referenced in the Why Buy Statement; this is step 2 when building an ROI Value Matrix.

CBT computer-based training.

consultative sale consultative selling means a sales professional 1) analyzes, understands, and confirms a buyer's unique business environment and operations, including issues, challenges, and goals, and its cost of status quo; 2) prescribes ways to improve the buyer's business by reducing costs, avoiding costs, and/or increasing revenue; and 3) assists the buyer to make an informed decision about purchasing the seller's goods or services.

CRM (Customer Resource Management) an application that supports your customer base; typically, it includes sales force automation (SFA), call center, dispatch, and contact management.

due diligence stage step 6 in our sample sales process, in which your customer or prospect confirms you are capable of delivering the value you estimated in the proposal and ROI model.

feature dumps a sales technique in which the sales professional or sales support specialist literally identifies all of a product's features (or service's capabilities); often this technique only succeeds in putting most in the buyer's audience to sleep.

GAAP generally accepted accounting principles.

investment the cost for your solution; typically the investment is displayed on the ROI Financial Dashboard.

IPO initial public offering; funds received for selling stock in a corporation.

KPI (key pain indicator) describes a primary issue, pain, or goal your customer or prospect experiences; a KPI is a restatement of the business issues identified in the ROI Workshop as questions designed to force a prospect to describe the pain they feel as a result of the issues.

marketing criteria the questions that a company must answer with a minimum quantifiable response before we consider them as a qualified buyer of our products/services.

meet and greet step 3 in your sales process, in which you meet your prospect either face-to-face or via teleconference; during this step, you will typically try to identify the key pain indicators.

needs analysis questionnaire the document within an ROI model that includes questions, benefits, and impacts on a customer's or prospect's business.

numbers game a term used to describe a belief that sales results are purely tied to numbers—for example, 100 calls results in 15 qualified prospects, which results in 2 sales; therefore, the more calls a sales professional makes, the more qualified leads he or she will develop, and the more sales he or she will make; selling is just a numbers game.

payback period the time it takes to recoup your investment.

PCI linkage the common buyer information connections between sales process phases and sales tools—defining the PCI connections ensures a logical progression of prospect-information gathering throughout the sales process.

pending sale stage 7 in our sample sales process, in which your prospect is validating the impact statements, typically through reference checks.

process connections information (PCI) common prospective customer information that links sales phase activities and sales tools; sales tools are sources and uses of PCI.

proposal a seller's written offer to a buyer to exchange property, goods, or services for money.

proposal stage a very important step in the sales process, in which you formally present the investment, cost, and value you expect to deliver.

qualify step 2 in the sales process, in which you identify the KPIs and confirm that they are worth pursuing.

revenue increase an act that caused an increase in bottom-line revenue that may or may not lead to an increase in profit.

ROI (return on investment) accumulated net benefits over a fixed period of time, divided by your initial cost; typically, the ROI is presented as a percentage.

ROI deliverable the tools that make up your ROI model; they include: needs analysis questionnaire, ROI Financial Dashboard, and the 360-degree value assessment model.

ROI Financial Dashboard a summary of calculations taken from the needs analysis questionnaire graphically displayed and summarized on one sheet.

ROI model the final version of the ROI deliverable.

ROI questionnaire needs analysis questionnaire made up of quantifiable questions to be used throughout the sales process.

ROI valuation tool a questionnaire designed to capture critical business issues, current costs, and estimated value delivered; typically, an ROI valuation tool includes financial metrics to assist a person in making a buying decision that include: net present value (NPV), internal rate of return (IRR), and/or ROI and payback period.

sales input form a version of the needs analysis questionnaire with the mathematics, benefit statements, and impact statements removed; also, there are no calculations of value; this form is strictly used to gather ROI data and re-input it into the ROI model.

sales tools any document, form, or system that 1) directly supports a company's sales professionals in following its consultative sales methodology, and 2) provides the prospective customer with information on which to make an informed buying decision.

search engine an Internet research tool for finding Web sites and other material that is available on the Internet or a company's intranet.

SFA (sales force automation) a software tool used to track and drive the sales process.

target the first step in a sample sales process; typically a target is a list of companies that your sales personnel will pursue for qualifying into their pipeline.

TCO total cost of ownership.

tell and sell perhaps one of the favorite sales techniques for a nonconsultative salesperson; "Let me tell you all about this product (because I don't know what to ask this buyer)."

value justification using ROI in the sales process to prove you are delivering more than you are charging for a product or service.

VC (venture capital) typically, early-round investment funds in a new company.

Webcast *see* Web seminar.

Web seminar a seminar delivered to participants using the Internet for video and often audio, although some Web seminars use a telephone for audio.

white paper an authoritative report on a major issue; may be 1) written by a team of experts, 2) a government report outlining policy, or 3) a short treatise whose purpose is to educate industry customers.

Resources

Recommended Reading List

Anthony, Mitch. *Selling with Emotional Intelligence.* Kaplan, 2003.

Bosworth, Michael T. *CustomerCentric Selling.* McGraw-Hill, 2003.

Bosworth, Michael T. *Solution Selling.* Irwin, 1994.

Byron Concevitch, Bill. *Increasing the Odds.* Mindset, 2001.

Chapman, Merrill. *In Search of Stupidity.* Apress, 2003.

Eades, Keith M. *The New Solution Selling.* McGraw-Hill, 2003.

Gitomer, Jeffrey. *The Little Red Book of Selling.* Bard Press, 2004.

Kantin, Bob. *Sales Proposals Kit for Dummies.* Wiley, 2001.

Khalsa, Mahan. *Let's Get Real or Let's Not Play.* Franklin-Covey, 1999.

Konrath, Jill. *Selling to Big Companies.* Kaplan, 2005.

Laughlin, Chuck. *Samurai Selling.* St. Martin's Press, 1994.

Lee, Kendra. *Selling Against the Goal.* Kaplan, 2005.

Marone, Mark, and Seleste Lunsford. *Strategies That Win Sales.* Kaplan, 2005.

Nick, Michael J. *ROI Selling.* Kaplan, 2004.

Page, Rick. *Hope Is Not a Strategy.* Nautilus Press, 2003.

Rackham, Neil. *Major Account Sales Strategy.* McGraw-Hill, 1989.

Rackham, Neil. *SPIN Selling.* McGraw-Hill, 1988.

Rackham, Neil, and John DeVincentis. *Rethinking the Sales Force.* McGraw-Hill, 1999.

RoAne, Susan. *How to Work a Room.* Shapolsky, 2001.

Sanchez, Diane. *Selling Machine.* Time Business, 1999.

Shonka, Mark, and Dan Kosch. *Beyond Selling Value.* Kaplan, 2002.

Siebel, Tom. *Virtual Selling.* Free Press, 2002.

Stein, Dave. *How Winners Sell.* Kaplan, 2004.

Thull, Jeff. *Mastering the Complex Sale.* Wiley, 2003.

Trout, Jack. *Differentiate or Die.* Wiley, 2001.

Value Estimation ROI Tools

ROI4Sales Inc.   *www.roi4sales.com*

Sales Proposals

SalesProposals.com   *www.salesproposals.com*

Consultative Sales Methods and Training

CustomerCentric Selling   *www.customercentricsystems.com*
Integrity Systems   *www.integritysystems.com*
KLA Group   *www.klagroup.com*
Miller Heiman   *www.millerheiman.com*
Prime Sales   *www.primeresource.com*
Richardson   *www.richardson.com*
Selling to Big Companies   *www.sellingtobigcompanies.com*
Solution Selling   *www.spisales.com*
SPIN Selling   *www.hulthwaite.com*
Value Selling   *www.valueselling.com*

CRM/SFA Systems

Aplicor   *www.aplicor.com*
Frontrange   *www.frontrange.com*
Microsoft   *www.microsoft.com*
Sage CRM   *www.sagesoftware.com*
Salesboom   *www.salesboom.com*

Salesforce.com	*www.salesforce.com*
SalesLogix	*www.saleslogix.com*
Salesnet	*www.salesnet.com*
SAP	*www.SAP.com*
Siebel (Oracle) Systems	*www.siebel.com*
SofFront	*www.soffront.com*
Sugar CRM	*www.sugarcrm.com*

Configuration Systems

| Endeavor Commerce | *www.endeavorcommerce.com* |
| Web Source | *www.webcominc.com* |

Lead Generation

Buyer Zone	*www.buyerszone.com*
D & B	*www.zapdata.com*
Edgar Scan	*www.edgarscan.pwcglobal.com*
Emailhunter.net	*www.emailhunter.net*
Factiva	*www.factiva.com*
First Research	*www.firstresearch.com*
Guaranteed Lists	*www.guaranteedlists.com*
Hoovers	*www.hoovers.com*
Intouch Inc.	*www.startwithalead.com*
Jigsaw	*www.jigsaw.com*
Market Makers	*www.marketmakers.com*
OneSource	*www.onesource.com*

Rainmaker Partners   *www.rainmaker-partners.com*
Sales Factory UK   *www.salesfactory.co.uk*
Sales Genie–Info USA   *www.salesgenie.com*
SSM   *www.manageyourleads.com*
Turner Marketing   *www.telemarketing-businesses.com*

Media, Newsletters, and Professional Organizations

CIO   *www.cio.com*
Line 56 Magazine   *www.line56.com*
Netbriefings   *www.netbriefings.com*
Optimize   *www.optimize.com*
Progressive Business   *www.pbp.com*
Sales and Marketing   *www.salesandmarketing.com*
  Management
SalesRepRadio.com   *www.salesrepradio.com*
SAMA   *www.strategicaccounts.org*
Selling Power   *www.sellingpower.com*
Selling to Big Companies   *www.sellingtobigcompanies.com*
Software Business   *www.webcom.com*
SoftwareCEO   *www.softwareceo.com*
Soundview Executive Book   *www.soundview.com*
  Summaries
SPIN Selling Newsletter   *www.huthwaite.com/thespin*

Research Resources

Bitpipe	*www.bitpipe.com*
Broadlook Corporation	*www.broadlook.com*
Cape Horn Strategies	*www.capehornstrategies.com*
CEO Express	*www.ceoexpress.com*
CSO Insights	*www.csoinsights.com*
Executive Link	*www.executive-link.com*
FinListics	*www.finlistics.com*
First Research	*www.firstresearch.com*
Gartner Group	*www.gartner.com*
HR Chally	*www.chally.com*
Softletter	*www.softletter.com*
Tower Group	*www.towergroup.com*
Ventana Research	*www.ventanaresearch.com*

Sales Intelligence Automation

Involve Technologies	*www.involvetechnology.com*

Contact Sharing

Contact Network	*www.contactnetworkcorp.com*
LinkedIN	*www.linkedin.com*

Marketing Strategy

TechVentive	*www.techventive.com*

Hiring and Testing

Bigby Havis & Associates	*www.bigby.com*
Caliper	*www.caliperonline.com*
Career Builder	*www.careerbuilder.com*
CraftSystems	*www.craftsystems.com*
Headway	*www.headwaycorp.com*
HR Chally	*www.chally.com*
IntelligentHire	*www.intelligenthire.com*
Salestestonline	*www.salestestonline.com*

Other Sales Productivity Products

Cardscan	*www.cardscan.com*
Convoqs (Web meetings)	*www.convoqs.com*
Free 411	*800-free-411 (800-473-3411)*
Glance	*www.glance.net*
Go to Meeting	*www.gotomeeting.com*
Macromedia	*www.macromedia.com*
National Association of Sales Persons	*www.nasp.com*
Proficient (watch users on your Web site)	*www.proficient.com*
Research in Motion	*www.rim.com*
Sales Roundup	*www.salesroundup.com*
Sales Spider	*www.salesspider.com*
Web Ex	*www.webex.com*
Why Johnny Can't Sell	*www.whyjohnnycantsell.com*

Public Golf Courses
(Entertaining Clients . . . Yeah, Right!)

Bandon Dunes	*www.bandondunesgolf.com*
Bethpage State Park Golf Course	*www.nysparks.com*
Pacific Dunes	*www.bandondunesgolf.com*
Pebble Beach Golf Links	*www.pebblebeach.com*
Pinehurst Resort and CC (#2)	*www.pinehurst.com*
Shadow Creek	*www.shadowcreek.com*
The Ocean Course	*www.kiawahgolf.com*
Whistling Straits G.C. (Straits)	*www.whistlingstraits.com*

Index

Share the message!

Bulk discounts
Discounts start at only 10 copies and range from 30% to 55% off retail price based on quantity.

Custom publishing
Private label a cover with your organization's name and logo. Or, tailor information to your needs with a custom pamphlet that highlights specific chapters.

Ancillaries
Workshop outlines, videos, and other products are available on select titles.

Dynamic speakers
Engaging authors are available to share their expertise and insight at your event.

Call Kaplan Publishing Corporate Sales at 1-800-621-9621, ext. 4444, or e-mail kaplanpubsales@kaplan.com

PUBLISHING